W9-ADB-383

Working on the Reports

- Provide a variety of resources for student research—nonfiction library books, bookmarked Internet sites, etc. Utilize the expertise of your school librarian if you are fortunate to have one.

- Set aside adequate classroom time to work on the reports so you can monitor student progress and pull small groups who need specific assistance.

- The final copy of most of the reports should be completed on unlined paper. To help students write neatly and in a straight line, make up a class set of lined templates:

  - Take one sheet of ruled paper (the kind students use every day).
  - Trace over each line using a ruler and a fine-tipped black marker.
  - Photocopy a class set.
  - Laminate.

  Students paper-clip blank paper on top of the template. The lines show through to guide their writing.

- Help students proofread their reports before completing a final copy. A proofreading checklist is provided on page 238. If you wish, this checklist may be mounted on construction paper and laminated for permanency.

- Some reports require students to list resources used in a bibliography. On page 239, you will find a chart showing how to write bibliographic entries for several types of resources. Reproduce this guide for each student or laminate and post for student reference.

Completing and Displaying the Report

- Glue the completed report cover to the outside of the folder.
- For reports that have minibooks, staple the pages to the report form.
- Glue reproducibles in place inside the folder.
- Display the report opened flat with the 3-D visual in its place.

A Word About Research Skills

The ability and experience level of your class will determine how much teaching or reviewing of research skills is needed. These reports will be more successful if your class has practiced research strategies, note-taking skills, and bibliography entries.

Do not expect students to be able to locate and synthesize information without repeated instruction and practice. If your students are new to research and reporting skills, we suggest doing several file folder reports as a class, with you modeling and guiding research strategies and note-taking using reference materials you have chosen.

3-D Visuals

Different types of 3-D visuals enhance the appeal of *Easy File Folder Reports*. Specific directions are provided here for pipe-cleaner people, stand-up visuals, and pop-up visuals.

Pipe-Cleaner People

These engaging visuals are easy to make and pose. Pipe-cleaner people may be dressed in construction paper, fabric, aluminum foil, doll clothes, or a combination of materials. The people may be dressed in class or completed at home. It's a good family project.

Pipe-cleaner people can be posed in any position, performing any feat—dancing, sitting, jumping, and even standing on their heads!

You will want to practice making a pipe-cleaner person yourself before guiding students through the process. Give directions one step at a time; don't go on to the next step until everyone is ready. Caution children not to bend the "people" too many times—they start to look "strange."

Depending on the age and ability of your group, you may want to make several finished samples yourself to provide completion ideas.

1 Use the first pipe cleaner to create the head and arms. Twist around to create the neck.

2 Use the second pipe cleaner to create the torso and legs. Wrap around the twisted part of the first pipe cleaner.

3 Twist the pipe cleaner to create the rest of the body shape. Twist at the waist; bend out the feet and hands.

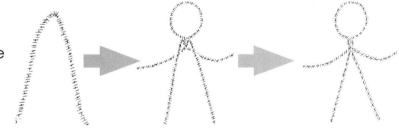

They're Easy!

You get everything you need to guarantee great results.

For the teacher:

- detailed directions for each report
- background notes on the topic
- list of topics for each report theme
- materials list for every report

For the students:

- Step-by-step directions
- Easy-to-complete report forms
- A polished, finished product that promotes a feeling of success
- The simple, structured format allows each student to complete reports at his or her skill level.
- Everyone does an individual report on a different topic within a theme.
- With writing, drawing, and constructing, the reports appeal to many learning styles.
- Each report features a 3-D visual that students will love making and displaying.

Helpful Hints for Successful Reports

Materials

- All reports fit into a letter-size file folder. Gather used file folders from the school office; ask friends and family who work in the business world to recycle their old file folders through you. In lieu of file folders, 12" x 18" (30.5 x 46 cm) sheets of construction paper may be used.

- A number of reports use a piece of cardboard as the base for holding the 3-D visual. Save sturdy boxes that can be cut up for this purpose.

- A classroom craft box full of material scraps, straws toothpicks, rafia, yarn, glitter, paint, and all sorts of fun add-ons can make the 3-D stand-up displays extra special.

- Common classroom supplies such as glue, scissors, crayons, etc., are **not** listed for each project.

Assigning the Reports

All reports will be individualized. A list of topic ideas for most themes appears at the end of each report section.

You may assign the report in several ways:

- let students choose their topics
- you assign each topic
- have students pick a topic out of a hat
- assign reports alphabetically

Introducing the Reports

- Explain the report theme to students and provide background information that may motivate student writing.

- Discuss each step of the student directions with your students, modeling where appropriate. Assess understanding of each section before going on. Explain that the box in front of each step is for them to check off each completed step.

- Make overhead transparencies of the reproducible forms for each report. Display them on the screen as you go over the directions, pointing to each section as it is explained.

- Have students fill in the date by which the report is to be completed.

- Depending on the language skills of your class, you may wish to make a list of words that might be needed in writing about the topic.

- With younger or less skilled groups, you may want to introduce and complete one section of the report at a time.

    Easy File Folder Reports • EMC 6001 • ©2004 by Evan-Moor Corp.

Use paper, fabric, and odds and ends to create the character.

Add a ball of clay to the feet. Shape it into shoes or boots.

Place glue on the bottom of each shoe and place on the cardboard. Balance it until it dries.

Stand-up Visuals

Stand-up visuals can be created from a variety of materials. Students may use recycled cartons, boxes, cardboard, or file folders. These projects are fun to do and stimulate creative thinking. The activity is most successful if there is a wide variety of craft materials for the students to use. Parents may contribute to a craft center in the room where all sorts of interesting things may be chosen to add to these visuals:

- yarn
- cotton
- stickers
- ribbon

- tinfoil
- foam fabric
- tongue depressors
- old thread spools

- toothpicks
- paper tubes
- foam core
- fabric

File Folder Stand-ups

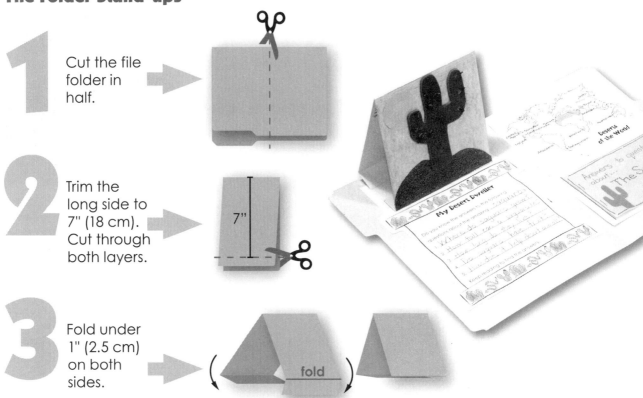

1 Cut the file folder in half.

2 Trim the long side to 7" (18 cm). Cut through both layers.

3 Fold under 1" (2.5 cm) on both sides.

7"

fold

Use construction paper and craft materials to create a picture of the topic. Glue the images to the file folder stand-up.

When students add a stand-up visual to a file folder report, they glue down the front folded lip in the area designated on the report reproducible. The stand-up picture can then be laid down when the folder is closed.

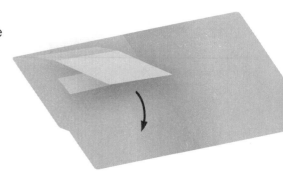

Slice and Slip Stand-ups

1 Cut two objects from lightweight cardboard or tagboard.

2 Slice one shape up from the bottom. Slice the other shape down from the top.

3 Slip one over the other and stand it up.

4 Glue the bottom to a piece of cardboard.

Flagpole Stand-ups

1 Fold the construction paper strip in half and design the flag.

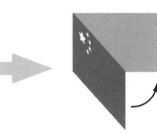

2 Place the skewer inside the fold and glue the two sides of the paper together.

3 Punch a hole in the cardboard and insert skewer. Add a drop of glue to secure.

Pop-up Visuals

Follow these steps to create pop-up visuals from **reproducible forms** provided in projects:

1 With the printed side facing out, fold the page in half along the line. Cut through both layers of the paper along the dotted lines.

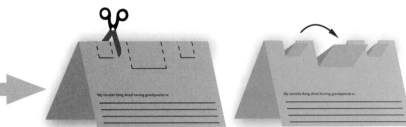

2 Open the page. Refold the paper so that the printed side is inside. Gently pull the cut tab into the center, reversing the folds. Carefully close the pop-up on itself and press firmly to establish new fold lines. Open the pop-up and apply glue to the front of the pop-up tab. Affix the pop-up art.

3 Create a folder for the pop-up from an 8½" x 11" (21.5 x 28 cm) sheet of construction paper. Lay the folded pop-up in the folder. Apply glue to the back of the pop-up page and press the folder closed. Flip the folder over. Open the cover and apply glue to the back of the other side of the pop-up page. Close the folder and press firmly.

Follow these steps to create pop-up visuals from **plain construction paper:**

1. Fold the paper in half. Cut a tab along the fold.

2. Gently pull the cut tab into the center, reversing the folds. Carefully close the pop-up on itself and press firmly to establish new fold lines.

3. Open the pop-up and apply glue to the front of the pop-up tab. Affix the pop-up art. Glue the pop-up onto a folded piece of construction paper as described above.

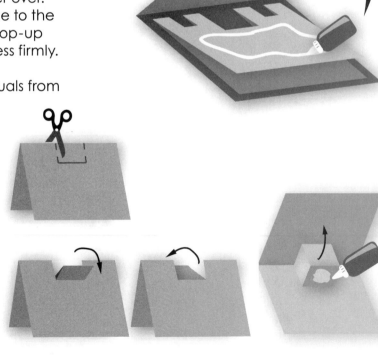

Contents

All About Me

What better way to begin the school year! This report gives all students a chance to express themselves and to let others know their special qualities. The finished projects generate classroom conversations about individual uniqueness. They also help to produce a class "team" of individuals who know and understand each other and are thus better able to work together.

This report is also an excellent memory of the school year for your class. It is sure to go in the box of "keepers" that come home from school.

Decide when to assign the homework sheet (page 17). The homework sheet must be completed and returned to school before you can proceed.

Before Assigning the Report

1. Prepare the following materials for each student:

   • student direction sheets on pages 12 and 13

   • report reproducibles on pages 14–16

   • homework reproducible on page 17

   • for the pipe-cleaner person:
     – 4" (10 cm) square piece of cardboard
     – 2 pipe cleaners
     – a variety of materials to dress and finish the pipe-cleaner person (see page 4)

2. Check each student's homework sheet for completeness before beginning the report.

Completing the Report

1. Distribute materials to students.

2. Introduce the report following the guidelines and suggestions on page 2.

3. Guide students step by step to make the pipe-cleaner person (see page 4).

4. Follow the guidelines on page 3 for assisting students as they work on and complete the report.

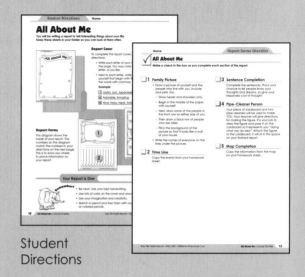

Student Directions

Report Reproducibles

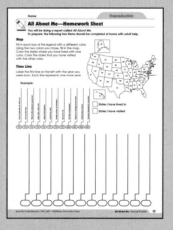

Homework Reproducible

All About Me

You will be writing a report to tell interesting things about your life. Keep these sheets in your folder so you can look at them often.

Report Cover

To complete the report cover, follow these directions:

- Write each letter of your name vertically on the page. You may color or decorate each letter, as you like.

- Next to each letter, write words describing yourself that begin with that letter. Separate the words with commas. Capitalize them all.

Example:

J   Joyful, Just, Japanese

A   Adorable, Amazing

N   Nice, Noisy, Neat, Noble

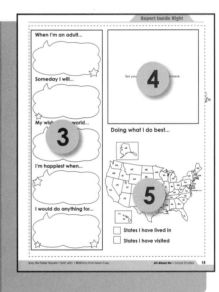

Report Forms

This diagram shows the inside of your report. The numbers on the diagram match the numbers in your directions on the next page. This is to show you where to place information on your report.

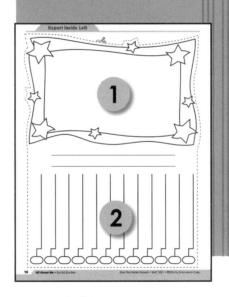

Your Report Is Due

Remember!

- Be neat. Use your best handwriting.
- Use lots of color on the cover and around the borders.
- Use your imagination and creativity.
- Sketch in pencil and then finish with markers, crayons, or colored pencils.

All About Me

Make a check in the box as you complete each section of the report.

1 Family Picture

- Draw a picture of yourself and the people who live with you. Include your pets, too.
    - Draw heads and shoulders only.
    - Begin in the middle of the paper with yourself.
    - Next, draw some of the people in the front row on either side of you.
    - Then draw a back row of people who are taller.
    - Fill in the background of the picture so that it looks like a wall of your house.
- Write the names of everyone on the lines under the picture.

2 Time Line

Copy the events from your homework sheet.

3 Sentence Completion

Complete the sentences. This is your chance to let people know your thoughts and dreams, so give your responses a lot of thought.

4 Pipe-Cleaner Person

Your piece of cardboard and two pipe cleaners will be used to make YOU. Your teacher will give directions for making the figure. It is your job to dress the figure and pose it on the cardboard so it represents you "doing what you do best." Attach the figure to the cardboard; it will sit in this space on your finished report.

5 Map Completion

Copy the information from the map on your homework sheet.

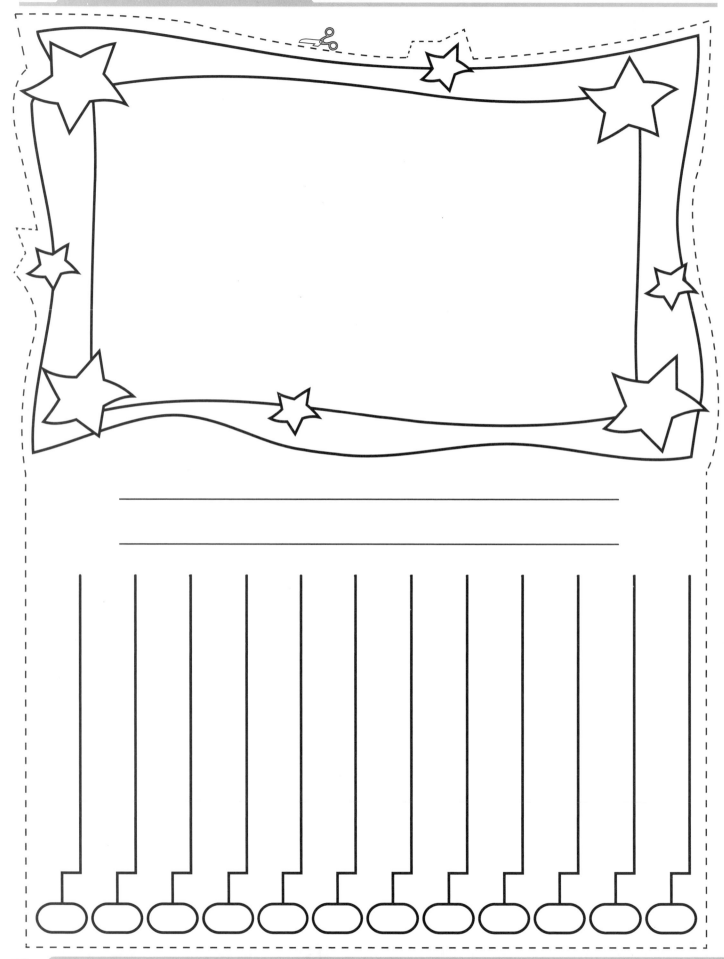

When I'm an adult...

Set your pipe-cleaner person here.

Someday I will...

My wish for the world...

Doing what I do best...

I'm happiest when...

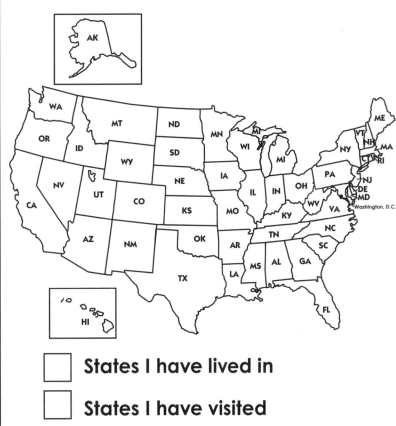

I would do anything for...

☐ States I have lived in

☐ States I have visited

All About Me

Easy File Folder Reports • EMC 6001 • ©2004 by Evan-Moor Corp.

All About Me—Homework Sheet

**You will be doing a report called *All About Me*.
Please ask your parents to help you fill out this information.**

Map

Fill in each box of the legend with a different color.
Using the two colors you chose, fill in the map.
Color the states where you have lived with one
color. Color the states that you have visited
with the other color.

Time Line

Label the first line on the left with the year you
were born. Each line represents one more year.

Example:

Born in Nashville, TN, 8:03 a.m.	Took my first step	Went to Miss Barbara's preschool	Baby sister, Sally, born	Started kindergarten	Learned to swim	Family reunion at Grandpa's	Moved to CA	First trip to Disneyland	Played on winning soccer team	Started piano lessons	Became interested in volcanoes
1992	1993	1994	1995	1996	1997	1998	1999	2000	2001	2002	2003

☐ States I have lived in

☐ States I have visited

Whether to set foot on untouched land or to discover a plant or animal no one has ever seen, humans are fascinated by the idea of going where no one has gone before. The report topics on page 25 present a variety of explorers, and encourage students to expand their view of explorers beyond the "Age of Exploration" of the 15th and 16th centuries.

Explorers

Easy File Folder Reports • EMC 6001 • ©2004 by Evan-Moor Corp.

Before Assigning the Report

1. Prepare the following materials for each student:

   - student direction sheets on pages 20 and 21

   - report reproducibles on pages 22–24

   - 6 sheets of plain white paper, cut 4" x 7" (10 x 18 cm)

   - 5 index cards for note-taking

   - any small container: school milk carton, paper tube, box or foam container for creating the explorer's mode of transportation

   - craft materials: construction paper, glue, craft sticks, scissors, chenille stems, etc.

2. Decide how to assign the reports. (See the directions on page 2 and the list of explorers on page 25.)

Completing the Report

1. Distribute materials to students.

2. Introduce the report following the guidelines and suggestions on page 2.

3. Discuss how to write a "first person" narrative. This report will be written as if the students were writing about a firsthand experience.

4. Follow the guidelines on page 3 for assisting students as they work on and complete the report.

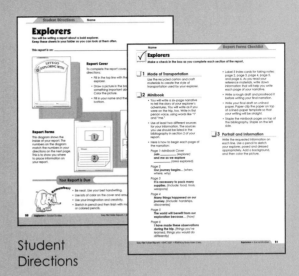

Student Directions

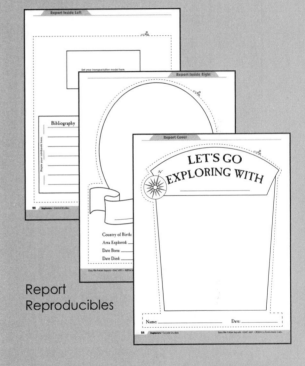

Report Reproducibles

Explorers Reproducible

Explorers

You will be writing a report about a bold explorer.
Keep these sheets in your folder so you can look at them often.

This report is on: _____

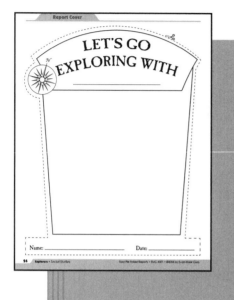

Report Cover

To complete the report cover, follow these directions:

- Fill in the top line with the name of your explorer.

- Draw a picture in the box. It should show something important about the explorer. Color the picture.

- Fill in your name and the date at the bottom.

Report Forms

This diagram shows the inside of your report. The numbers on the diagram match the numbers in your directions on the next page. This is to show you where to place information on your report.

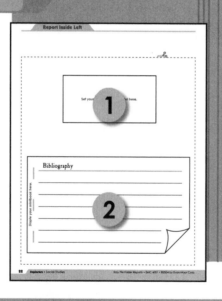

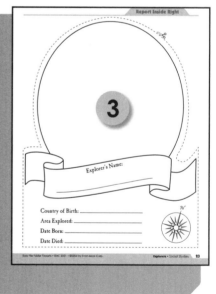

Your Report Is Due

- Be neat. Use your best handwriting.
- Use lots of color on the cover and around the borders.
- Use your imagination and creativity.
- Sketch in pencil and then finish with markers, crayons, or colored pencils.

Explorers

Make a check in the box as you complete each section of the report.

1 Mode of Transportation

Use the recycled carton and craft materials to create the style of transportation used by your explorer.

2 Minibook

- You will write a six-page narrative to tell the story of your explorer's adventures. You will write as if you were on the trip, too. Write in first person voice, using words like "I" and "me."

- Use at least two different sources for your information. The sources you use should be listed in the bibliography in section 2 of your report.

- Here is how to begin each page of the narration:

Page 1–Minibook Cover
   Write: **Join** _____ *(explorer)* **and me as we explore** _____ *(area explored)*.

Page 2
   Our journey begins... *(when, where, why)*

Page 3
   It is necessary to pack many supplies. *(Include: food, tools, weapons)*

Page 4
   Many things happened on our journey. *(Include: hardships, discoveries)*

Page 5
   The world will benefit from our exploration because... *(how)*

Page 6
   I have made these observations during the trip. *(things you've learned, things you would do differently)*

- Label 5 index cards for taking notes: page 2, page 3, page 4, page 5, and page 6. As you read your reference materials, write down information that will help you write each page of your narrative.

- Write a rough draft and proofread it before writing your final narration.

- Write your final draft on unlined paper. Paper-clip the paper on top of a lined-paper template so that your writing will be straight.

- Staple the minibook pages on top of the bibliography. Staple on the left side.

3 Portrait and Information

Write the requested information on each line. Use a pencil to sketch your explorer, posed and dressed appropriately. Add a background, and then color the picture.

Set your transportation model here.

Bibliography

Staple your minibook here.

Explorer's Name:

Country of Birth: _____

Area Explored: _____

Date Born: _____

Date Died: _____

𝒩

LET'S GO EXPLORING WITH

_____

Name: _____ Date: _____

Explorers

Alexander the Great	King of Macedonia (356–323 B.C.)
Roald Amundsen	first to reach the South Pole (1911)
Neil A. Armstrong	first person to walk on the moon (1969)
Charles William Beebe	first to descend 3,028 ft. below sea level in a bathysphere (1934)
Daniel Boone	cleared the Wilderness Road (1771)
Robert Burke	made first north/south crossing of Australia (1861)
James Bridger	discovered the Great Salt Lake (1824)
Richard E. Byrd	explored Antarctica (1925)
William Clark	reached the Pacific Northwest (1805)
Captain James Cook	explored the St. Lawrence River and Pacific Ocean (1750s)
Jacques Cousteau	underwater explorer (1910–1997)
Charles Darwin	explored South America (1831)
Amelia Earhart	first woman to fly solo across the Atlantic Ocean (1932)
Yuri Gagarin	first man in space (1961)
Vasco da Gama	discovered sea route to India by way of Cape of Good Hope (1498)
John Glenn	first American to orbit Earth (1962)
Henry Hudson	explored the Hudson River (1610)
Henry the Navigator	explored West Africa for Portugal (1419)
Matthew Henson	reached the North Pole with Peary (1908)
Alexander von Humboldt	geographer; explored South America (1799)
Amy Johnson	first woman to fly solo from England to Australia (1930)
Mary Kingsley	first woman explorer of Africa (1880s)
Meriwether Lewis	reached the Pacific Northwest (1805)
Charles Lindbergh	first solo nonstop transatlantic flight (1927)
David Livingston	great British explorer of Africa (1870s)
Ferdinand Magellan	first successful voyage around the world (1519)
Robert Peary	Arctic explorer who reached the North Pole (1909)
Marco Polo	Italian traveler who became famous for his travels in central Asia and China
Valentina Tereshkova	first woman to orbit Earth (1963)

Native Americans

Many distinct groups of Native Americans were living in the United States, Canada, and Mexico when European explorers and settlers first came to the New World in the 16th and 17th centuries. As they research, students will discover fascinating information and come to appreciate and respect the uniqueness of these native groups.

...if you lived with the Cheyenne Indians

...if you lived with The Cheyenne Indians

This is where you lived in America...

This is how you dressed...

Before Assigning the Report

1. Prepare the following materials for each student:

   - student direction sheets on pages 28 and 29

   - report reproducibles on pages 30–33

   - 10 sheets of plain white paper, cut 4" x 7" (10 x 18 cm)

   - 10 index cards for note-taking

   - an assortment of materials for making native dwellings: cloth, leather, twigs, craft sticks, boxes, tortillas, etc. Encourage students to brainstorm choices for materials and help them to gather items they need.

2. Decide how to assign the reports. (See the directions on page 2 and the list of tribes on pages 34 and 35.)

Completing the Report

1. Distribute materials to students.

2. Introduce the report following the guidelines and suggestions on page 2.

3. Follow the guidelines on page 3 for assisting students as they work on and complete the report.

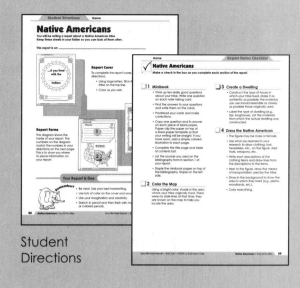

Student Directions

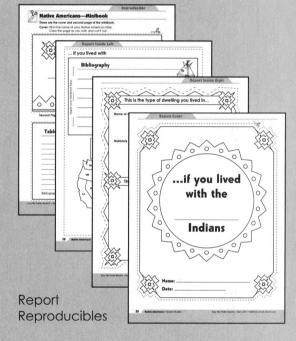

Report Reproducibles

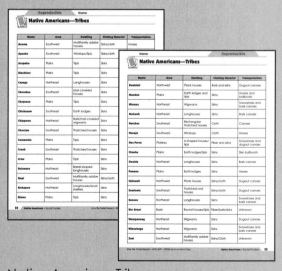

Native American Tribes Reproducibles

Native Americans

You will be writing a report about a Native American tribe.
Keep these sheets in your folder so you can look at them often.

This report is on: _____

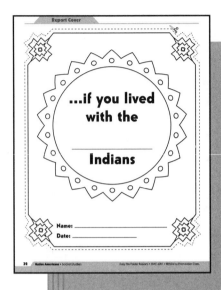

Report Cover

To complete the report cover, follow these directions:

- Using large letters, fill in the name of your tribe on the top line.

- Color as you wish.

Report Forms

This diagram shows the inside of your report. The numbers on the diagram match the numbers in your directions on the next page. This is to show you where to place information on your report.

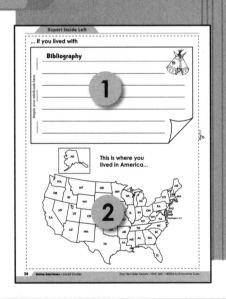

Your Report Is Due _____

- Be neat. Use your best handwriting.
- Use lots of color on the cover and around the borders.
- Use your imagination and creativity.
- Sketch in pencil and then finish with markers, crayons, or colored pencils.

Native Americans

Make a check in the box as you complete each section of the report.

1 Minibook

- Think up ten really good questions about your tribe. Write one question on each note-taking card.

- Find the answers to your questions and write them on the cards.

- Proofread your cards and make corrections.

- Copy one question and its answer on each piece of blank paper. Paper-clip the paper on top of a lined-paper template so that your writing will be straight. If you have room, add a simple colored illustration to each page.

- Complete the title page and table of contents last.

- List the sources you used on the bibliography form in section 1 of your report.

- Staple the minibook pages on top of the bibliography. Staple on the left side.

2 Color the Map

Using a bright color, shade in the area where your tribe originally lived. There were no state lines at that time; they are shown on the map to help you locate the area.

3 Create a Dwelling

- Construct the type of house in which your tribe lived. Make it as authentic as possible; the materials you use should resemble as closely as possible those originally used.

- Label the type of dwelling (e.g., tipi, longhouse). List the materials from which the actual dwelling was constructed.

4 Dress the Native American

- The figure may be male or female.

- Use what you learned in your research to draw clothing, hair, headdress, etc., on the figure. Add tools, weapons, etc.

- Write short descriptions of the clothing items and draw lines from the descriptions to the items.

- Next to the figure, draw the means of transportation used by the tribe.

- Draw in the background to show the area in which they lived (e.g., plains, woodlands, etc.).

- Color everything.

... if you lived with

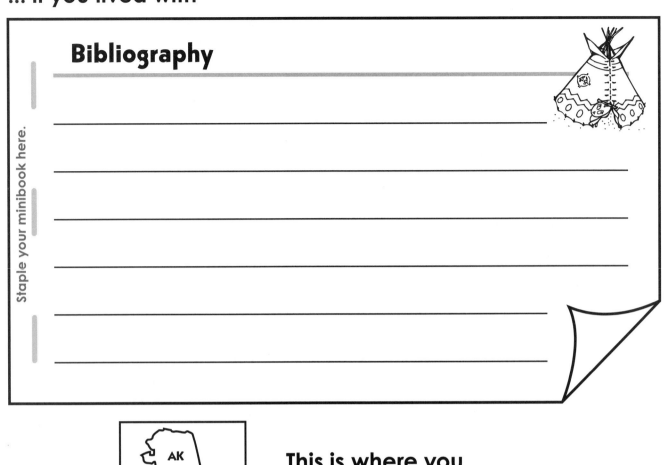

Bibliography

Staple your minibook here.

This is where you
lived in America...

This is the type of dwelling you lived in...

Name of dwelling:

Set your dwelling piece here.

Materials used:

This is how you dressed...

...if you lived with the

_____

Indians

Name: _____

Date: _____

Easy File Folder Reports • EMC 6001 • ©2004 by Evan-Moor Corp

Reproducible

Native Americans—Minibook

These are the cover and second page of the minibook.

Cover: Fill in the name of your Native American tribe.
Color the page as you wish and cut it out.

The

_____

Indians

Second Page: Write each of the ten questions about your tribe on a line.
Be sure to number the report pages in the same order.

Table of Contents

          page

_____ 1

_____ 2

_____ 3

_____ 4

_____ 5

_____ 6

_____ 7

_____ 8

_____ 9

_____ 10

Bibliography _____ 11

Native Americans—Tribes

Name	Area	Dwelling	Clothing Material	Transportation
Acoma	Southwest	Multifamily adobe houses	Skins/cloth	Horses
Apache	Southwest	Wickiups/tipis	Skins/cloth	Horses
Arapaho	Plains	Tipis	Skins	Horses
Blackfeet	Plains	Tipis	Skins	Horses
Cayuga	Northeast	Longhouses	Skins	Bark canoes
Cherokee	Southeast	Mat-covered houses	Skins	Dugout canoes
Cheyenne	Plains	Tipis	Skins	Horses
Chickasaw	Southeast	Earth lodges	Skins	Dugout canoes
Chippewa	Northeast	Bark/mat-covered wigwams	Skins	Snowshoes and bark canoes
Choctaw	Southeast	Thatched houses	Skins	Dugout canoes
Comanche	Plains	Tipis	Skins	Horses
Creek	Southeast	Thatched houses	Skins	Dugout canoes
Crow	Plains	Tipis	Skins	Skin boats and horses
Delaware	Northeast	Barrel-shaped longhouses	Skins	Dugout canoes
Hopi	Southwest	Multifamily adobe houses	Skins/cloth	Unknown
Kickapoo	Northeast	Longhouses/brush shelters	Skins	Horses
Kiowa	Plains	Tipis	Skins	Horses

Native Americans—Tribes

Name	Area	Dwelling	Clothing Material	Transportation
Kwakiutl	Northwest	Plank houses	Bark and skins	Dugout canoes
Mandan	Plains	Earth lodges and tipis	Skins	Horses and bullboats
Micmac	Northeast	Wigwams	Skins	Snowshoes and bark canoes
Mohawk	Northeast	Longhouses	Skins	Bark canoes
Natchez	Southeast	Rectangular thatched houses	Cloth	Canoes
Navajo	Southwest	Wickiups	Cloth	Horses
Nez Perce	Plateau	A-shaped houses/ tipis	Fiber and skins	Snowshoes and dugout canoes
Omaha	Plains	Earth lodges/tipis	Skins	Skin bullboats
Oneida	Northeast	Longhouses	Skins	Bark canoes
Pawnee	Plains	Earth lodges	Skins	Horses
Quinault	Northwest	Plank houses	Skins/cloth	Dugout canoes
Seminole	Southeast	Thatched-roof houses	Skins/cloth	Dugout canoes
Seneca	Northeast	Longhouses	Skins	Snowshoes and bark canoes
Ute Great	Basin	Round houses/tipis	Fiber/bark/skins	Unknown
Wampanoag	Northeast	Wigwams	Skins	Dugout canoes
Winnebago	Northeast	Wigwams	Skins	Snowshoes and bark canoes
Zuni	Southwest	Multifamily adobe houses	Skins/Cloth	Unknown

This report will familiarize students with women whose accomplishments have made a difference in our world. Traditionally, men have outnumbered women eleven to one in elementary and secondary school history textbooks. The study of women's lives and roles can give students a broader understanding and appreciation of American history. Through sharing their projects, students will become familiar with many important women.

Women of America

Before Assigning the Report

1. Prepare the following materials for each student:

   - student direction sheets on pages 38 and 39

   - report reproducibles on pages 40–42

   - for the pipe-cleaner person:
     – 4" (10 cm) square piece of cardboard or foam core
     – 2 pipe cleaners
     – a variety of materials to dress and finish the pipe-cleaner person (see page 4)

   - 6 sheets of plain white paper, cut 4" x 7" (10 x 18 cm)

   - 5 index cards for note-taking

2. Decide how to assign the reports. (See the directions on page 2 and the list of Women of America on page 43.)

Completing the Report

1. Distribute materials to students.

2. Introduce the report following the guidelines and suggestions on page 2.

3. Guide students step by step to make the pipe-cleaner person (see page 4).

4. Follow the guidelines on page 3 for assisting students as they work on and complete the report.

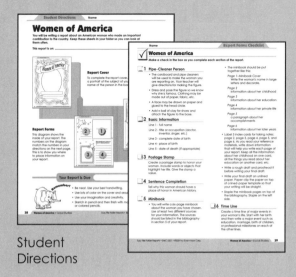

Student Directions

Report Reproducibles

Women of America Reproducible

Women of America

You will be writing a report about an American woman who made an important contribution to the country. Keep these sheets in your folder so you can look at them often.

This report is on: _____

Report Cover

To complete the report cover, draw and color a portrait of the subject of your report. Write the name of the person in the box.

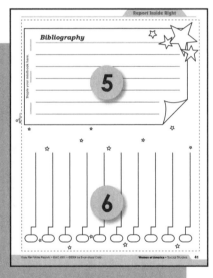

Report Forms

This diagram shows the inside of your report. The numbers on the diagram match the numbers in your directions on the next page. This is to show you where to place information on your report.

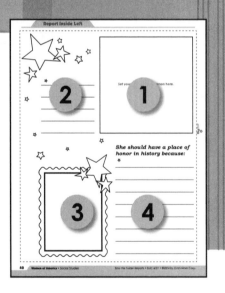

Your Report Is Due

Remember!

- Be neat. Use your best handwriting.
- Use lots of color on the cover and around the borders.
- Use your imagination and creativity.
- Sketch in pencil and then finish with markers, crayons, or colored pencils.

Women of America

Make a check in the box as you complete each section of the report.

1 Pipe-Cleaner Person

- The cardboard and pipe cleaners will be used to make the woman you are reporting on. Your teacher will give directions for making the figure.

- Dress and pose the figure so we know why she is famous. Clothing may be made out of paper, fabric, etc.

- A face may be drawn on paper and glued to the head circle.

- Add a ball of clay for shoes and attach the figure to the base.

2 Basic Information

Line 1 - full name

Line 2 - title or occupation (doctor, inventor, singer, etc.)

Line 3 - complete date of birth

Line 4 - place of birth

Line 5 - date of death (if appropriate)

3 Postage Stamp

Create a postage stamp to honor your woman. Include words or objects that highlight her life. Give the stamp a value.

4 Sentence Completion

Tell why this woman should have a place of honor in American history.

5 Minibook

- You will write a six-page minibook about the woman you have chosen. Use at least two different sources for your information. The sources should be listed in the bibliography in section 5 of your report.

- The minibook should be put together like this:

  Page 1–Minibook Cover
  Write the woman's name in large letters and decorate.

  Page 2
  information about her childhood

  Page 3
  information about her education

  Page 4
  information about her private life

  Page 5
  a paragraph about her accomplishments

  Page 6
  information about her later years

- Label 5 index cards for taking notes: page 2, page 3, page 4, page 5, and page 6. As you read your reference materials, write down information that will help you write each page of your report. Keep all the information about her childhood on one card, all the things you read about her education on another card, etc.

- Write a rough draft and proofread it before writing your final draft.

- Write your final draft on unlined paper. Paper-clip the paper on top of a lined-paper template so that your writing will be straight.

- Staple the minibook pages on top of the bibliography. Staple on the left side.

6 Time Line

Create a time line of major events in your woman's life. Start with her birth and then write a major event such as education, marriage, birth of children, or professional milestones on each of the other lines.

Set your pipe-cleaner person here.

She should have a place of honor in history because:

_____

_____

_____

_____

_____

_____

_____

_____

Easy File Folder Reports • EMC 6001 • ©2004 by Evan-Moor Corp.

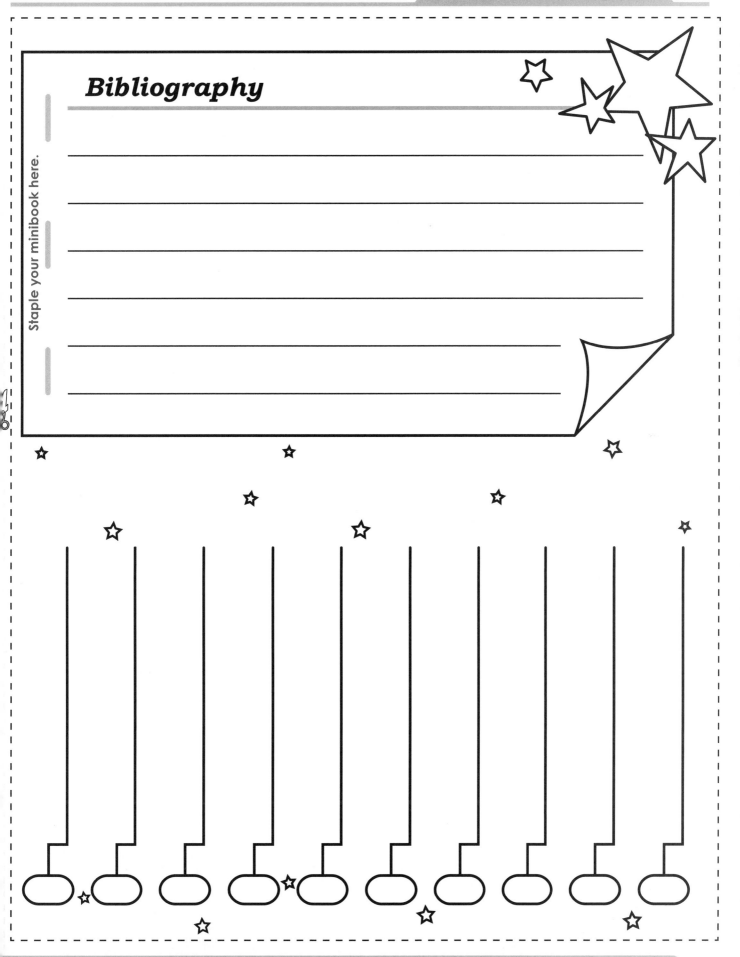

Bibliography

Staple your minibook here.

Women of America

Name: _____

Date: _____

Women of America

Jane Addams	first American woman to win the Nobel Peace Prize
Marian Anderson	first Black American to sing with the Metropolitan Opera
Susan B. Anthony	woman suffragist
Clara Barton	founder of the American Red Cross
Mary McLeod Bethune	teacher; first Black woman to head a federal agency
Elizabeth Blackwell	first woman doctor of medicine in modern times
Laura Bridgman	first blind, deaf-mute person to be taught
Pearl S. Buck	first American woman to win the Nobel Prize for literature
Rachel Carson	environmentalist who wrote *The Silent Spring*
Isadora Duncan	dancer
Amelia Earhart	first woman to fly across the Atlantic Ocean
Dolores Huerta	vice president of the United Farm Workers Union
Emma Lazarus	wrote poem entitled "The New Colossus," now inscribed on a plaque at the base of the Statue of Liberty
Juliette Gordon Low	founded Girl Scouts of America
Mae Jemison	first Black woman astronaut
Susanna Madora	first woman elected mayor of a U.S. city
Margaret Mead	anthropologist
Maria Mitchell	first American woman astronomer and discoverer of a comet
Sandra Day O'Connor	first woman associate justice of the U.S. Supreme Court
Georgia O'Keeffe	contemporary American artist
Libby Riddles	first woman to win 1,000-mile Iditarod Trail Sled Dog Race
Sally Ride	first American woman astronaut
Eleanor Roosevelt	most famous First Lady; great humanitarian
Wilma Rudolph	Olympic gold medal runner
Sacajawea	Lewis and Clark's guide through the West
Harriet Beecher Stowe	author of *Uncle Tom's Cabin*
Maria Tallchief	greatest ballerina born in America
Harriet Tubman	former slave who escorted slaves to freedom on the Underground Railroad
Phillis Wheatley	first Black woman poet to be published
Jade Snow Wong	artist; pottery maker; writer
Victoria Woodhull	first woman to run for president of the U.S.

Black Americans

Black Americans have contributed much to this country. Historically, however, their contributions have not received adequate acknowledgement. By completing this report, students will become familiar with some of these men and women whose endeavors in government, science, the arts, and sports have left a lasting legacy. In sharing the information they acquire, students may develop an awareness of the qualities of character common to those who have made a difference in the world.

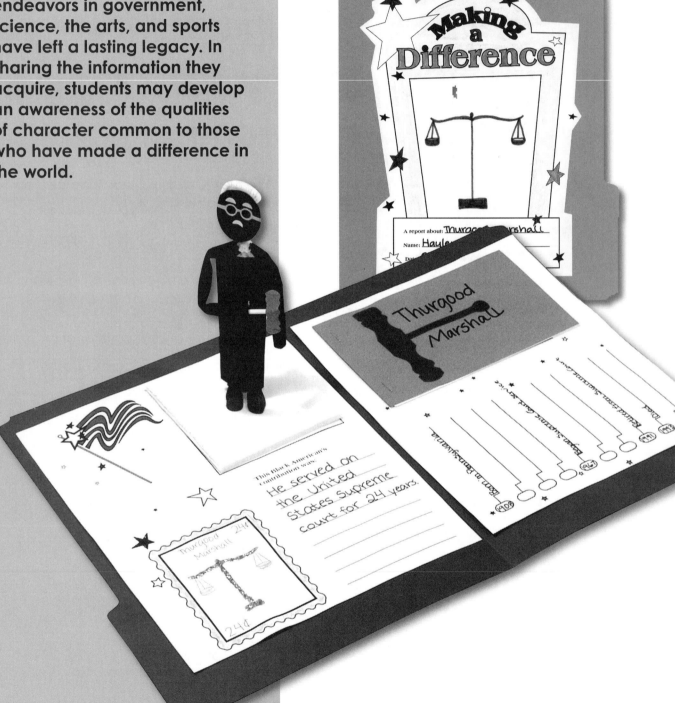

Easy File Folder Reports • EMC 6001 • ©2004 by Evan-Moor Corp.

Before Assigning the Report

1. Prepare the following materials for each student:

    - student direction sheets on pages 46 and 47

    - report reproducibles on pages 48–50

    - for the pipe-cleaner person:
        - 4" (10 cm) square piece of cardboard
        - 2 pipe cleaners
        - a variety of materials to dress and finish the pipe-cleaner person (see page 4)

    - 6 sheets of plain white paper, cut 4" x 7" (10 x 18 cm)

    - 5 index cards for note-taking

2. Decide how to assign the reports. (See the directions on page 2 and the list of Black Americans on page 51.)

Completing the Report

1. Distribute materials to students.

2. Introduce the report following the guidelines and suggestions on pages 2.

3. Guide students step by step to make the pipe-cleaner person (see page 4).

4. Follow the guidelines on page 3 for assisting students as they work on and complete the report.

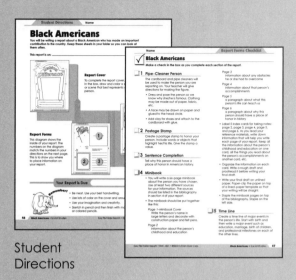

Student Directions

Report Reproducibles

Black Americans Reproducible

Black Americans

You will be writing a report about a Black American who has made an important contribution to the country. Keep these sheets in your folder so you can look at them often.

This report is on: _____

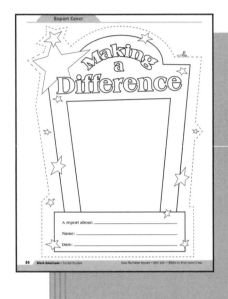

Report Cover

To complete the report cover, fill in the lines. In the box, draw and color a symbol, object, or scene that best represents your famous person.

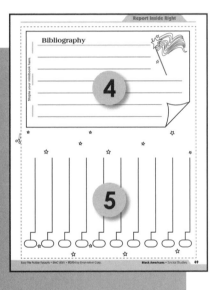

Report Forms

This diagram shows the inside of your report. The numbers on the diagram match the numbers in your directions on the next page. This is to show you where to place information on your report.

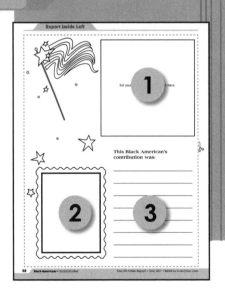

Your Report Is Due

Remember!

- Be neat. Use your best handwriting.
- Use lots of color on the cover and around the borders.
- Use your imagination and creativity.
- Sketch in pencil and then finish with markers, crayons, or colored pencils.

Name

 # Black Americans

Make a check in the box as you complete each section of the report.

1 Pipe-Cleaner Person

The cardboard and pipe cleaners will be used to make the person you are reporting on. Your teacher will give directions for making the figure.

- Dress and pose the person so we know why she/he is famous. Clothing may be made out of paper, fabric, etc.

- A face may be drawn on paper and glued to the head circle.

- Add clay for shoes and attach to the cardboard with glue.

2 Postage Stamp

Create a postage stamp to honor your person. Include words or objects that highlight her/his life. Give the stamp a value.

3 Sentence Completion

Tell why this person should have a place of honor in American history.

4 Minibook

- You will write a six-page minibook about the person you have chosen. Use at least two different sources for your information. The sources should be listed in the bibliography in section 4 of your report.

- The minibook should be put together like this:

Page 1–Minibook Cover
Write the person's name in large letters and decorate with construction paper and felt pens.

Page 2
information about the person's childhood and education

Page 3
information about any obstacles he or she had to overcome

Page 4
information about that person's accomplishments

Page 5
a paragraph about what this person's life can teach us

Page 6
a paragraph about why this person should have a place of honor in history

- Label 5 index cards for taking notes: page 2, page 3, page 4, page 5, and page 6. As you read your reference materials, write down information that will help you write each page of your report. Keep all the information about the person's childhood and education on one card, all the things you read about the person's accomplishments on another card, etc.

- Organize the information on each card. Write a rough draft and proofread it before writing your final draft.

- Write your final draft on unlined paper. Paper-clip the paper on top of a lined-paper template so that your writing will be straight.

- Staple the minibook pages on top of the bibliography. Staple on the left side.

5 Time Line

Create a time line of major events in the person's life. Start with birth and then write a major event such as education, marriage, birth of children, and professional milestones on each of the other lines.

Set your pipe-cleaner person here.

This Black American's contribution was:

_____

_____

_____

_____

_____

_____

_____

_____

   Easy File Folder Reports • EMC 6001 • ©2004 by Evan-Moor Corp.

Bibliography

Staple your minibook here.

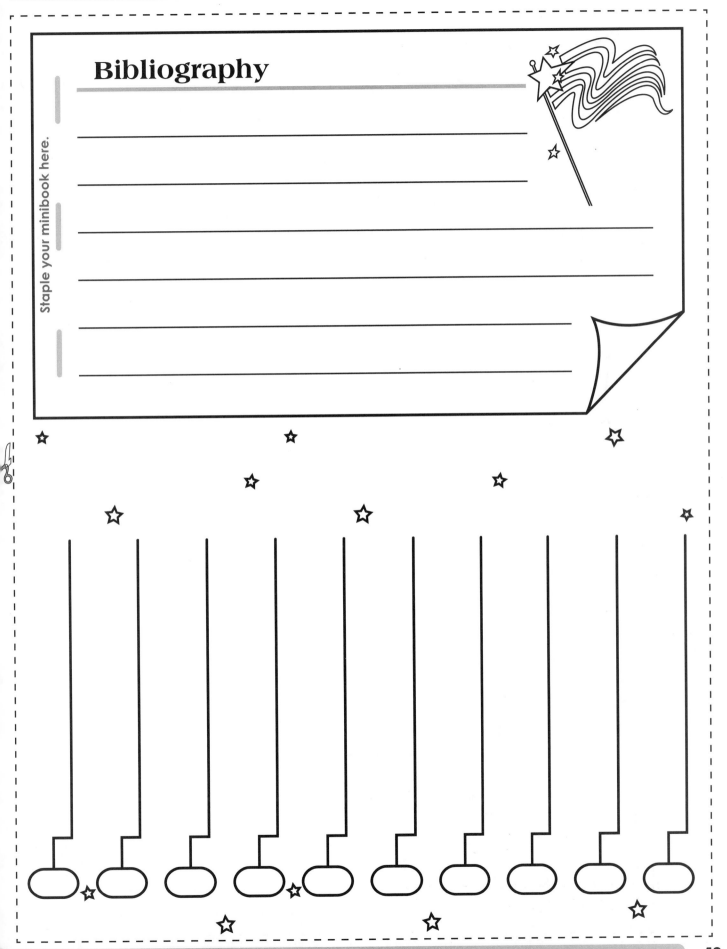

Making a **Difference**

A report about: _____

Name: _____

Date: _____

   Easy File Folder Reports • EMC 6001 • ©2004 by Evan-Moor Corp.

Black Americans

Henry (Hank) Aaron	baseball superstar; broke Babe Ruth's home run record
Muhammad Ali	boxing champion
Marian Anderson	opera contralto
Maya Angelou	poet; educator; author
Louis Armstrong	musician
Crispus Attuks	patriot; died in the Boston Massacre
Benjamin Banneker	scientist; helped design plans for Washington, D.C.
Gwendolyn Brooks	poet (1950 Pulitzer Prize)
Ralph Bunche	statesman and diplomat (Nobel Peace Prize)
George W. Carver	botanist and educator in scientific agriculture
Shirley Chisolm	first Black woman elected to Congress
Charles Drew	medical researcher; surgeon; organized blood banks
W. E. B. Du Bois	historian; sociologist; founded the NAACP
Frederick Douglass	abolitionist
Paul Lawrence Dunbar	poet
Duke Ellington	musician
Alex Haley	writer
Matthew A. Henson	explorer; first man to reach the North Pole with Robert E. Peary
Jesse Jackson	minister and civil rights leader
Mahalia Jackson	gospel singer
Mae Jemison	first Black American woman astronaut
Scott Joplin	musician and composer
Michael Jordan	basketball player
Frederick M. Jones	invented the refrigerated truck
Martin Luther King, Jr.	clergyman and civil rights leader
Thurgood Marshall	first Black Supreme Court judge
Arthur Mitchell	director of the Dance Theater of Harlem
Jesse Owens	track-and-field athlete; Olympic medalist
Rosa Parks	civil rights activist
Colin L. Powell	Secretary of State
Leontyne Price	opera soprano
Jackie Robinson	baseball player; first Black in the major leagues
Wilma Rudolph	runner; Olympic medalist
Sojourner Truth	abolitionist
Harriet Tubman	abolitionist; started the Underground Railroad
Cicely Tyson	actress
James Va Der Zee	photographer
Booker T. Washington	educator
Oprah Winfrey	talk-show hostess; actress
Phillis Wheatley	poet
Tiger Woods	professional golfer
Andrew Young	U.S. ambassador to the United Nations

Incredible People

The people listed as subjects for this report may not be familiar to your students, but all have accomplished extraordinary feats in fields from science to the arts. Students will enjoy learning about people who are truly incredible. Display these reports for the school and community to see. Your students will be proud to show off their finished products.

Before Assigning the Report

1. Prepare the following materials for each student:

   - student direction sheets on pages 54 and 55

   - report reproducibles on pages 56–58

   - for the pipe-cleaner person:
     – 4" (10 cm) square piece of cardboard
     – 2 pipe cleaners
     – a variety of materials to dress and finish the pipe-cleaner person (see page 4)

   - index cards for note-taking

2. Decide how to assign the reports. (See the directions on page 2 and the list of incredible people on page 59.)

Completing the Report

1. Distribute materials to students.

2. Introduce the report following the guidelines and suggestions on page 2.

3. Guide students step by step to make the pipe-cleaner person (see page 4).

4. Students will write about their subject in the form of an encyclopedia article. Share with the class a number of short biographies from "kid-friendly" encyclopedias. Discuss the type of information found. Create a set of guidelines for students to use while doing their own research and writing.

5. Follow the guidelines on page 3 for assisting students as they work on and complete the report.

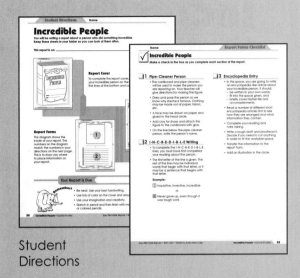

Student Directions

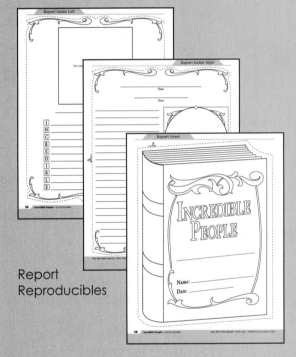

Report Reproducibles

Incredible People Reproducible

Incredible People

You will be writing a report about a person who did something incredible. Keep these sheets in your folder so you can look at them often.

This report is on: _____

Report Cover

To complete the report cover, write the name of your incredible person on the first line. Complete the lines at the bottom and color.

Report Forms

This diagram shows the inside of your report. The numbers on the diagram match the numbers in your directions on the next page. This is to show you where to place information on your report.

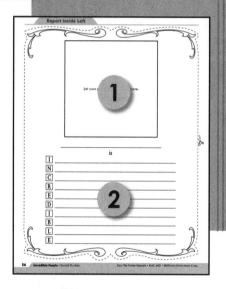

Your Report Is Due

Remember!

- Be neat. Use your best handwriting.
- Use lots of color on the cover and around the borders.
- Use your imagination and creativity.
- Sketch in pencil and then finish with markers, crayons, or colored pencils.

Incredible People

Make a check in the box as you complete each section of the report.

1 Pipe-Cleaner Person

- The cardboard and pipe cleaners will be used to make the person you are reporting on. Your teacher will give directions for making the figure.

- Dress and pose the person so we know why she/he is famous. Clothing may be made out of paper, fabric, etc.

- A face may be drawn on paper and glued to the head circle.

- Add clay for shoes and attach this figure to the cardboard with glue.

- On the line below the pipe-cleaner person, write the person's name.

2 I-N-C-R-E-D-I-B-L-E Writing

- To complete the I-N-C-R-E-D-I-B-L-E lines, you must have first completed your reading about the person.

- The first letter of the line is given. The rest of the line may be individual words that begin with that letter, or it may be a sentence that begins with that letter.

Example:

Ⓘ Inquisitive, Inventive, Incredible

or

Ⓝ Never gave up, even though it was tough work

3 Encyclopedia Entry

- In this space, you are going to write an encyclopedia-like article about your incredible person. It should:
  - be written in your own words,
  - fit into the space given, and
  - briefly cover his/her life and accomplishments.

- Read a number of different short encyclopedia articles first to see how they are arranged and what information they contain.

- Complete your reading and note-taking.

- Write a rough draft and proofread it. Decide if you need to cut anything in order to fit the available space.

- Transfer the information to the report form.

- Add an illustration in the circle.

Set your pipe-cleaner person here.

_____

is

I _____

N _____

C _____

R _____

E _____

D _____

I _____

B _____

L _____

E _____

_____
Name

_____
Dates

Name: _____

Date: _____

  Easy File Folder Reports • EMC 6001 • ©2004 by Evan-Moor Corp.

Incredible People

Jane Addams	founder of Hull House, the first community center
John James Audubon	painter of birds
Mikhail Baryshnikov	ballet superstar
Ludwig van Beethoven	famous composer
Louis Braille	invented "writing" for the blind
Cesar Chavez	spokesman for farm workers
Winston Churchill	led England during World War II
Marie Curie	Nobel Prize-winning scientist; discovered radium
Walt Disney	creator of Mickey Mouse
Thomas Alva Edison	inventor
Albert Einstein	brilliant scientist
Anne Frank	kept a famous diary while hiding from the Nazis
Benjamin Franklin	diplomat; inventor; master of many trades
Indira Gandhi	first woman prime minister of India
Mohandas Gandhi	nonviolent reformer; won freedom for India
Bill Gates	co-founder of world's largest software company
Johannes Gutenberg	father of printing
Janet Guthrie	daredevil auto racer
Helen Keller	blind and deaf woman who helped the disabled around the world
Joseph Rudyard Kipling	storyteller
Dorothea Lange	photographer
Aldo Leopold	father of the National Wilderness System
Maya Ying Lin	architect who designed the Vietnam Veterans Memorial
Margaret Mead	American anthropologist
Maria Montessori	teacher; started a unique way to teach children
Samuel F.B. Morse	invented the Morse Code
Anna "Grandma" Moses	American folk artist
John Muir	protector of the wilderness
Nikola Tesla	pioneer in electrical technology
Pelé	soccer superstar
Alfred Nobel	established the Nobel Prize award
Ringling Brothers	circus owners who founded "The Greatest Show on Earth"
Albert Schweitzer	missionary doctor
Levi Strauss	inventor of the blue jeans
Mother Teresa	cared for the "poorest of the poor" in India
Frank Lloyd Wright	famous and controversial American architect

National monuments are places of historic, scientific, or scenic interest set aside by the United States government as public property. They include structures, such as historic forts, and natural features, such as canyons.

This report is designed to familiarize students with the variety of monuments and the history behind them. When they are finished with this report, they will have experienced the next-best thing to actually being there! Through their research, they will also learn about our country's past—historically and geologically.

National Monuments & Memorials

Before Assigning the Report

1. Prepare the following materials for each student:

   - student direction sheets on pages 62 and 63
   - report reproducibles on pages 64–66
   - 4" x 7" (10 x 18 cm) piece of cardboard
   - a variety of resources that students may use to construct monuments—cardboard, tagboard, craft sticks, sugar cubes, soap bars, salt dough, papier-mâché, foam core, modeling clay, and other decorative materials
   - index cards for note-taking

2. Decide how to assign the reports. (See the directions on page 2 and the list of monuments and memorials on page 67.)

Completing the Report

1. Distribute materials to students.

2. Introduce the report following the guidelines and suggestions on page 2.

3. Present potential choices for construction materials for the monuments and memorials and demonstrate construction techniques.

4. Follow the guidelines on page 3 for assisting students as they work on and complete the report.

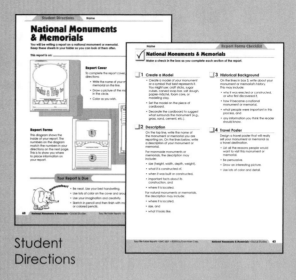

Student Directions

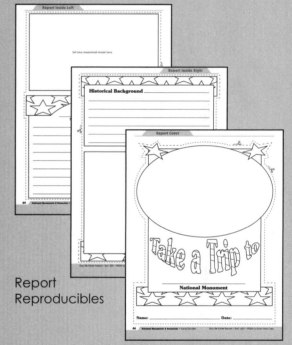

Report Reproducibles

National Monuments and Memorials Reproducible

National Monuments & Memorials

You will be writing a report on a national monument or memorial. Keep these sheets in your folder so you can look at them often.

This report is on: _____

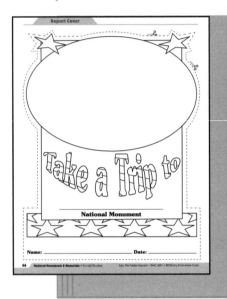

Report Cover

To complete the report cover, follow these directions:

- Write the name of your monument or memorial on the first line.

- Draw a picture of the monument or memorial in the circle.

- Color as you wish.

Report Forms

This diagram shows the inside of your report. The numbers on the diagram match the numbers in your directions on the next page. This is to show you where to place information on your report.

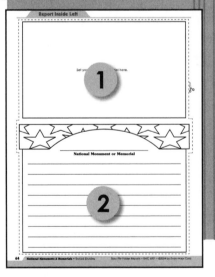

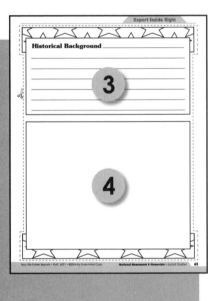

Your Report Is Due

- Be neat. Use your best handwriting.
- Use lots of color on the cover and around the borders.
- Use your imagination and creativity.
- Sketch in pencil and then finish with markers, crayons, or colored pencils.

National Monuments & Memorials

Make a check in the box as you complete each section of the report.

1 Create a Model

- Create a model of your monument or a symbol that best represents it. You might use: craft sticks, sugar cubes, carved soap bar, salt dough, papier-mâché, foam core, or modeling clay.

- Set the model on the piece of cardboard.

- Decorate the cardboard to suggest what surrounds the monument (e.g., grass, sand, cement, etc.).

2 Description

On the top line, write the name of the monument or memorial you are reporting on. On the lines below, write a description of your monument or memorial.

For manmade monuments or memorials, the description may include:

- size (height, width, depth, weight),

- what it is constructed of,

- when it was built or constructed,

- important facts about its construction, and

- where it is located.

For natural monuments or memorials, the description may include:

- where it is located,

- size, and

- what it looks like.

3 Historical Background

On the lines in box 3, write about your monument or memorial's history. This may include:

- why it was erected or constructed, or who first discovered it,

- how it became a national monument or memorial,

- what people were important in this process, and

- any information you think the reader should know.

4 Travel Poster

Design a travel poster that will really sell your monument or memorial as a travel destination.

- List all the reasons people would want to visit this monument or memorial.

- Be persuasive.

- Draw an interesting picture.

- Use lots of color and detail.

Set your monument model here.

_____

National Monument or Memorial

_____

_____

_____

_____

_____

_____

_____

_____

_____

Historical Background _____

_____

_____

_____

_____

_____

_____

Take a Trip to

National Monument

Name: _____   **Date:** _____

National Monuments and Memorials

Agate Fossil Beds (NE)	deposits of animal fossils
Arlington House (VA)	home of General Robert E. Lee
Bandelier (NM)	prehistoric Indian pueblo ruins
Cedar Breaks (UT)	huge natural amphitheater
Custer Battlefield (MT)	site of the Battle of Little Bighorn, 1876
Death Valley (CA, NV)	lowest spot in the Western Hemisphere
Devils Postpile (CA)	lava flow remains in 60-ft. (18-m) columns
Effigy Mounds (IA)	Indian mounds in shapes of bears/birds
Ford's Theatre (D.C.)	site of Abraham Lincoln's assassination
Fort Clatsop (OR)	winter campsite of Lewis & Clark
Fort Sumter (SC)	site of the beginning of the Civil War
Gettysburg (PA)	site of the Civil War battle that stopped the northern march of the Confederate Army
Golden Spike (UT)	completion of the first coast-to-coast railroad
Great Sand Dunes (CO)	largest, highest dunes in the U.S.
Homestead (NE)	first land claim under the Homestead Act
Jefferson Memorial (D.C.)	circular marble building with statue of the 3rd president
Johnstown Flood (PA)	memorial to the 3,000 people killed in the flood
Joshua Trees (CA)	Joshua trees
Lincoln Memorial (D.C.)	marble building with a statue of the 16th president
Mount Rushmore (SD)	carved heads of four presidents in granite cliff
Mount Saint Helens (WA)	established in 1982 as a National Volcanic Monument
Natural Bridges (UT)	three gigantic natural bridges of sandstone
Pipestone (MN)	stone quarry used by Native Americans
Rainbow Bridge (UT)	largest known natural bridge
Sequoia National Park (CA)	largest living thing on Earth (Sequoia tree)
Statue of Liberty (NY, NJ)	world's largest statue
Tomb of the Unknown Soldier (VA)	memorial to all soldiers killed in U.S. wars
Tonto (AZ)	Indian cliff dwellings dating to the 1300s
U.S.S. Arizona (HI)	floating memorial to the attack on Pearl Harbor, World War II
Washington Monument (D.C.)	555-ft.-tall (169-m) pillar honoring George Washington
White Sands (NM)	glistening white dunes of gypsum sand

U.S. States

The United States of America is one of the most diverse countries in the world—rich in natural resources, full of scenic wonders, and populated by people with varied cultural backgrounds. This report allows each student to take one state and look at its diversity and its historical place in the development of the nation. By studying the states and learning about our nation's past, students gain an understanding of our nation today.

Easy File Folder Reports • EMC 6001 • ©2004 by Evan-Moor Corp.

Before Assigning the Report

1. Prepare the following materials for each student:

   - student direction sheets on pages 70 and 71

   - report reproducibles on pages 72–74

   - 2½" (6.5 cm) square piece of cardboard

   - 10" (25 cm) bamboo skewer (sharp end cut off) or straw (for flagpole)

   - 1 piece of white paper, cut 3" x 8½" (7.5 x 21.5 cm) (for flag)

   - 7 sheets of plain white paper, cut 4" x 7" (10 x 18 cm)

   - index cards for note-taking

2. Decide how to assign the reports. (See the directions on page 2 and the list of states on page 75.)

Completing the Report

1. Distribute materials (except for modeling clay) to students.

2. Introduce the report following the guidelines and suggestions on page 2.

3. Follow the guidelines on page 3 for assisting students as they work on and complete the report.

4. Give each student enough modeling clay to support his/her flag on the piece of cardboard.

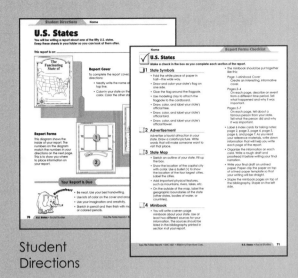

Student
Directions

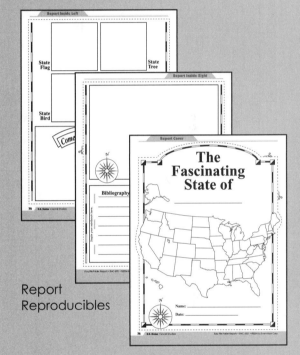

Report
Reproducibles

States and Capitals of the USA
Reproducible

U.S. States

You will be writing a report about one of the fifty U.S. states.
Keep these sheets in your folder so you can look at them often.

This report is on: _____

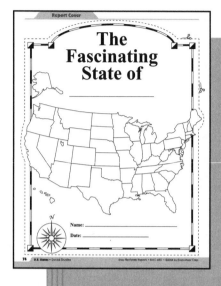

Report Cover

To complete the report cover, follow these directions:

- Neatly write the name of your state on the top line.

- Color in your state on the map using a bright color. Color the other states in a pale shade.

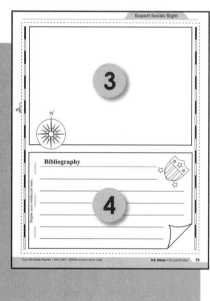

Report Forms

This diagram shows the inside of your report. The numbers on the diagram match the numbers in your directions on the next page. This is to show you where to place information on your report.

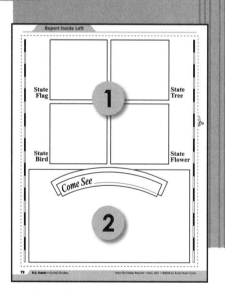

Your Report Is Due

Remember!

- Be neat. Use your best handwriting.
- Use lots of color on the cover and around the borders.
- Use your imagination and creativity.
- Sketch in pencil and then finish with markers, crayons, or colored pencils.

U.S. States

Make a check in the box as you complete each section of the report.

1 State Symbols

- Fold the white piece of paper in half—the wide way.
- Draw and color your state's flag on one side.
- Glue the flag around the flagpole.
- Use modeling clay to attach the flagpole to the cardboard.
- Draw, color, and label your state's official tree.
- Draw, color, and label your state's official bird.
- Draw, color, and label your state's official flower.

2 Advertisement

Advertise a tourist attraction in your state. Draw a colorful picture. Write words that will make someone want to visit that place.

3 State Map

- Sketch an outline of your state. Fill up the box.
- Show the location of the capital city with a star. Use a bullet (•) to show the location of the four largest cities. Label the cities.
- Add important physical features, such as mountains, rivers, lakes, etc.
- On the outside of the map, label the geographic boundaries of the state (other states, bodies of water, or countries).

4 Minibook

- You will write a seven-page minibook about your state. Use at least two different sources for your information. The sources should be listed in the bibliography printed in section 4 of your report.

- The minibook should be put together like this:

  Page 1–Minibook Cover
  Create an interesting, informative cover.

  Pages 2–4
  On each page, describe an event from a different time period. Tell what happened and why it was important.

  Pages 5–7
  On each page, tell about a famous person from your state. Tell what the person did and why it was important.

- Label 6 index cards for taking notes: page 2, page 3, page 4, page 5, page 6, and page 7. As you read your reference materials, write down information that will help you write each page of the report.

- Organize the information on each card. Write a rough draft and proofread it before writing your final narration.

- Write your final draft on unlined paper. Paper-clip the paper on top of a lined-paper template so that your writing will be straight.

- Staple the minibook pages on top of the bibliography. Staple on the left side.

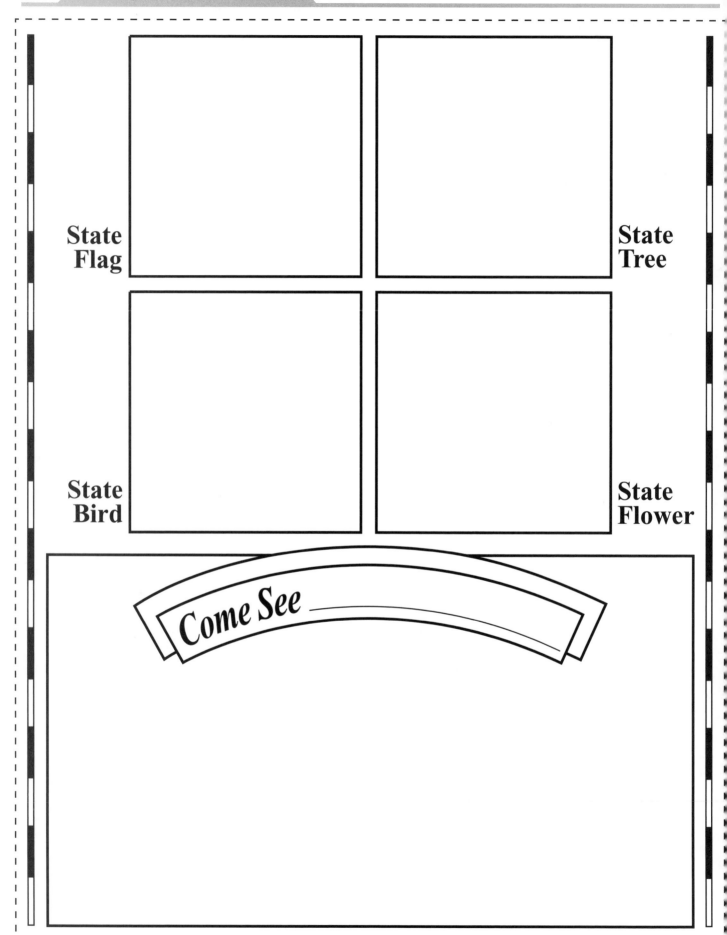

State Flag

State Tree

State Bird

State Flower

Come See

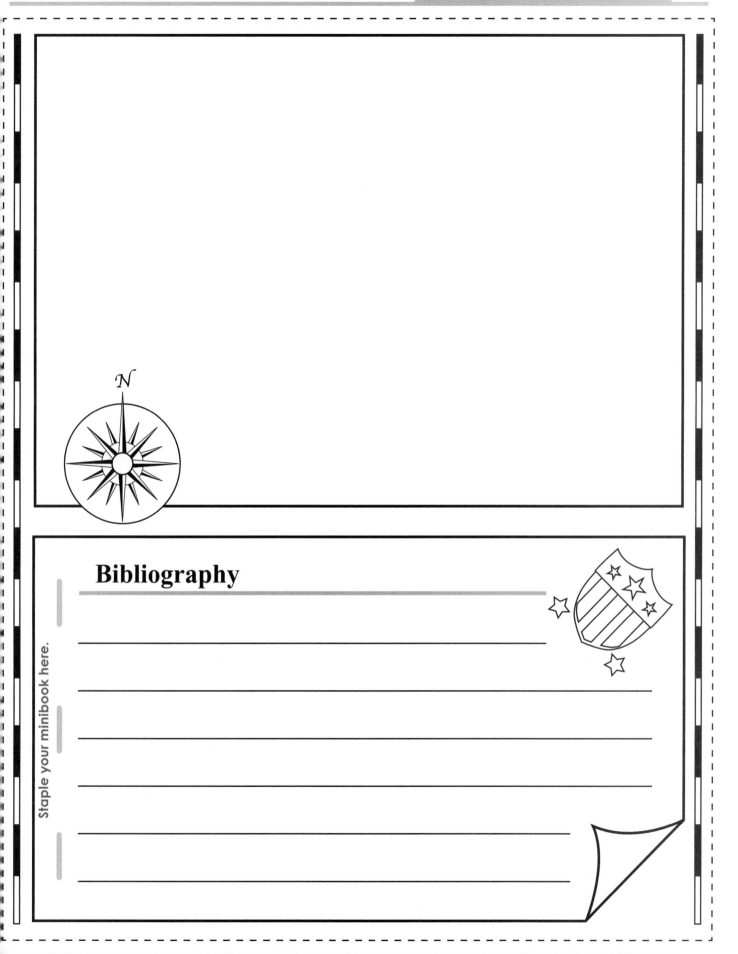

Bibliography

Staple your minibook here.

U.S. States • Social Studies

The Fascinating State of

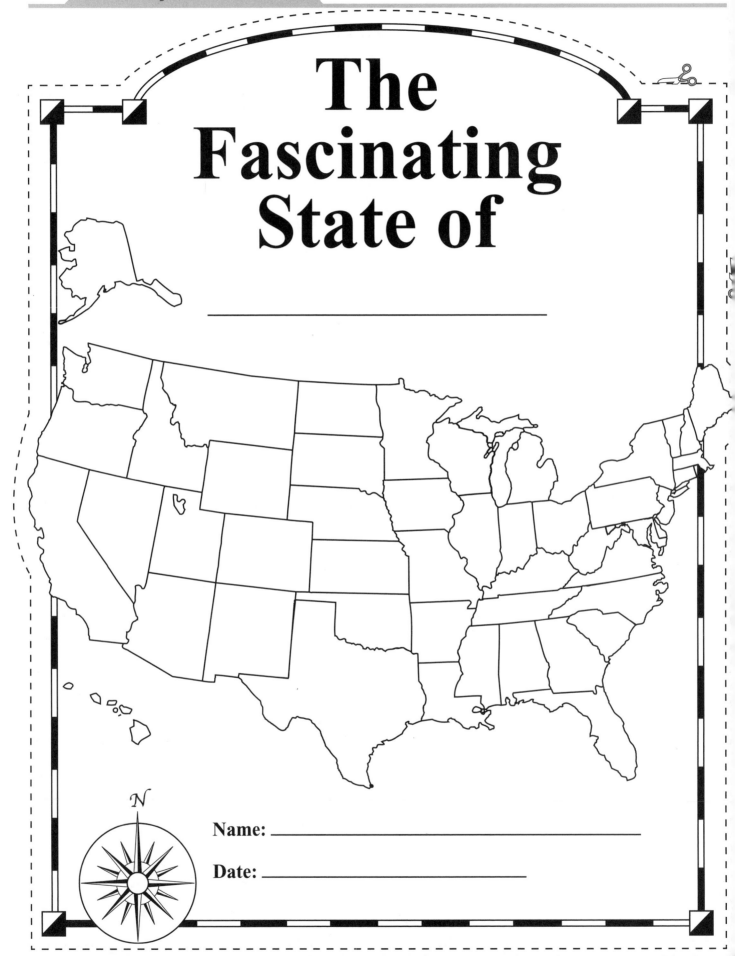

_____

Name: _____

Date: _____

States and Capitals of the USA

State	Capital
Alabama	Montgomery
Alaska	Juneau
Arizona	Phoenix
Arkansas	Little Rock
Colorado	Denver
California	Sacramento
Connecticut	Hartford
Delaware	Dover
Florida	Tallahassee
Georgia	Atlanta
Hawaii	Honolulu
Idaho	Boise
Illinois	Springfield
Indiana	Indianapolis
Iowa	Des Moines
Kansas	Topeka
Kentucky	Frankfort
Louisiana	Baton Rouge
Maine	Augusta
Maryland	Annapolis
Massachusetts	Boston
Michigan	Lansing
Minnesota	St. Paul
Mississippi	Jackson
Missouri	Jefferson City

State	Capital
Montana	Helena
Nebraska	Lincoln
Nevada	Carson City
New Hampshire	Concord
New Jersey	Trenton
New Mexico	Santa Fe
New York	Albany
North Carolina	Raleigh
North Dakota	Bismarck
Ohio	Columbus
Oklahoma	Oklahoma City
Oregon	Salem
Pennsylvania	Harrisburg
Rhode Island	Providence
South Carolina	Columbia
South Dakota	Pierre
Tennessee	Nashville
Texas	Austin
Utah	Salt Lake City
Vermont	Montpelier
Virginia	Richmond
Washington	Olympia
West Virginia	Charleston
Wisconsin	Madison
Wyoming	Cheyenne

U.S. Presidents

For over 200 years, it has been the most famous job in the world. Forty-three different men have held the office of President of the United States. Even though they have all shared the same title, their presidencies have been different in many ways.

By completing this report, students will become familiar with one president's role in shaping our country. As students share their reports and compare the various men who have held this important position, they will become more aware of human differences and the qualities leaders exhibit.

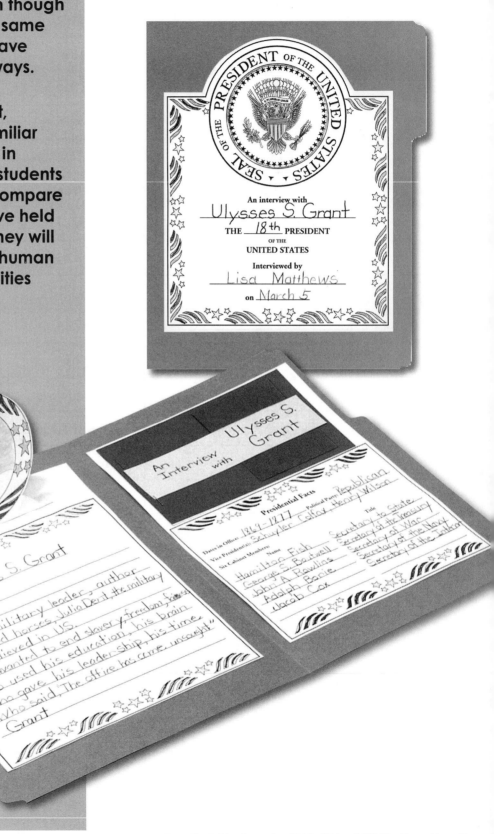

Easy File Folder Reports • EMC 6001 • ©2004 by Evan-Moor Corp.

Before Assigning the Report

1. Prepare the following materials for each student:

   - student direction sheets on pages 78 and 79
   - report reproducibles on pages 80–83
   - 7 or more sheets of plain white paper, cut 4" x 7" (10 x 18 cm)
   - index cards for note-taking

2. Decide how to assign the reports. (See the directions on page 2 and the list of presidents on page 84.)

Completing the Report

1. Distribute materials to students.

2. Introduce the report following the guidelines and suggestions on page 2.

3. Follow the guidelines on page 3 for assisting students as they work on and complete the report.

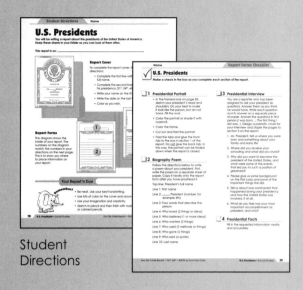

Student
Directions

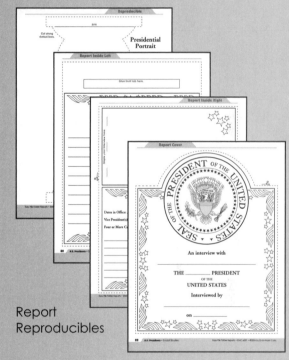

Report
Reproducibles

United States Presidents
Reproducible

U.S. Presidents

You will be writing a report about the presidents of the United States of America. Keep these sheets in your folder so you can look at them often.

This report is on: _____

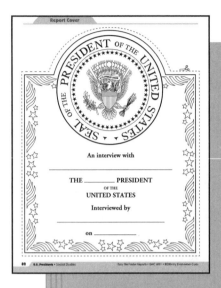

Report Cover

To complete the report cover, follow these directions:

- Complete the first line with your president's full name.
- Complete the second line with the order of his presidency (21st, 34th, etc.).
- Write your name on the third line.
- Write the date on the last line.
- Color as you wish.

Report Forms

This diagram shows the inside of your report. The numbers on the diagram match the numbers in your directions on the next page. This is to show you where to place information on your report.

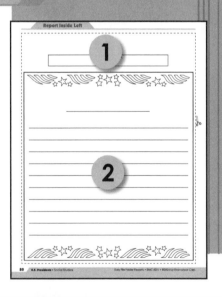

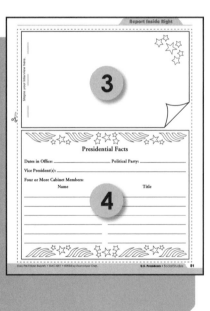

Your Report Is Due

Remember!

- Be neat. Use your best handwriting.
- Use lots of color on the cover and around the borders.
- Use your imagination and creativity.
- Sketch in pencil and then finish with markers, crayons, or colored pencils.

U.S. Presidents

Make a check in the box as you complete each section of the report.

1 Presidential Portrait

- In the framed oval on page 83, sketch your president's head and shoulders. Do your best to make it look like the person, but do not trace. Fill the oval.

- Color the portrait or shade it with a pencil.

- Color the frame.

- Cut out and fold the portrait.

- Fold the tabs and glue the front tab to the box in section 1 of the report. Do <u>not</u> glue the back tab. In this way, the portrait can be folded down when the report is closed.

2 Biography Poem

Follow the directions below to write a poem about your president. First, write the poem on a separate sheet of paper. Copy it neatly onto the report form after you have proofread it.

Top line: President's full name

Line 1: First name

Line 2: Write: _____ **President** (number—for example, 4th)

Line 3: Four words that describe the person

Line 4: **Who loved** (2 things or ideas)

Line 5: **Who believed** (1 or more ideas)

Line 6: **Who wanted** (2 things)

Line 7: **Who used** (2 methods or things)

Line 8: **Who gave** (2 things)

Line 9: **Who said** (a quote)

Line 10: Last name

3 Presidential Interview

You are a reporter who has been assigned to ask your president six questions. Answer them as you think he would have. Write each question and its answer on a separate piece of paper. Answer the questions in first person (*I was born…; The first thing I did was…*). Design a patriotic cover for your interview and staple the pages to section 3 on the report.

1. Mr. President, tell us where you were born and something about your family and early life.

2. Where did you receive your schooling and what did you study?

3. Why did you want to become the president of the United States, and what were some of the events that led you to such a position of greatness?

4. Please give us some background on the First Lady and some of the important things she did.

5. Tell us about one world event that happened during your presidency and how the United States was involved, if at all.

6. What do you feel was your most important accomplishment as president, and why?

4 Presidential Facts

Fill in the requested information neatly and accurately.

Glue front tab here.

Staple your interview here.

Presidential Facts

Dates in Office: _____   Political Party: _____

Vice President(s): _____

Four or More Cabinet Members:

Name   Title

_____   _____

_____   _____

_____   _____

_____   _____

_____   _____

_____   _____

An interview with

_____

THE _____ PRESIDENT

OF THE

UNITED STATES

Interviewed by

_____

on _____

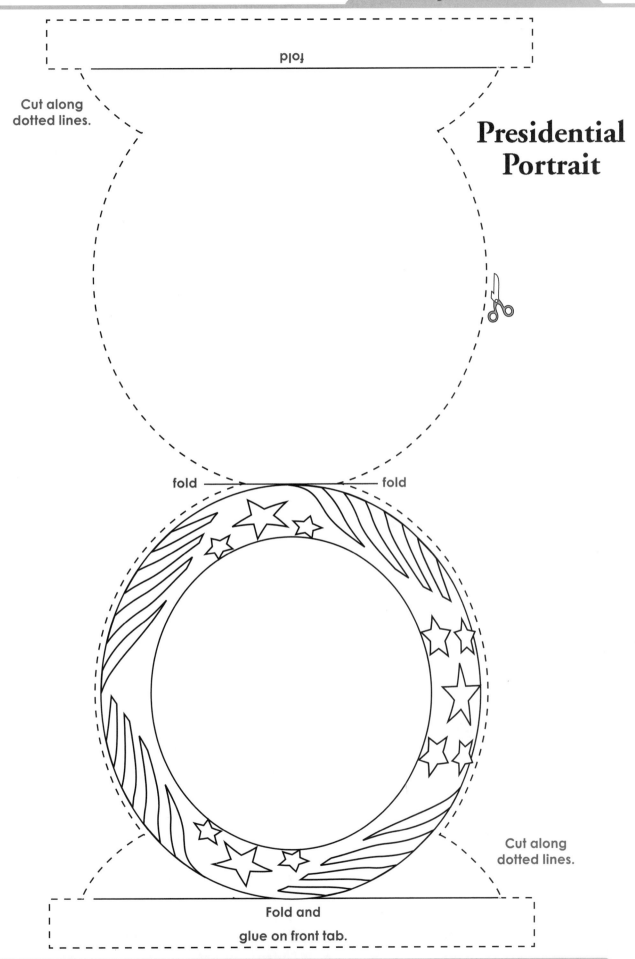

fold

Cut along
dotted lines.

Presidential
Portrait

fold —————— fold

Cut along
dotted lines.

Fold and

glue on front tab.

United States Presidents

1.	George Washington	1789–1797	Federalist
2.	John Adams	1797–1801	Federalist
3.	Thomas Jefferson	1801–1809	Democratic–Republican
4.	James Madison	1809–1817	Democratic–Republican
5.	James Monroe	1817–1825	Democratic–Republican
6.	John Quincy Adams	1825–1829	Democratic–Republican
7.	Andrew Jackson	1829–1837	Democrat
8.	Martin Van Buren	1837–1841	Democrat
9.	William H. Harrison	1841	Whig
10.	John Tyler	1841–1845	Whig
11.	James K. Polk	1845–1849	Democrat
12.	Zachary Taylor	1849–1850	Whig
13.	Millard Fillmore	1850–1853	Whig
14.	Franklin Pierce	1853–1857	Democrat
15.	James Buchanan	1857–1861	Democrat
16.	Abraham Lincoln	1861–1865	Republican
17.	Andrew Johnson	1865–1869	Democrat
18.	Ulysses S. Grant	1869–1877	Republican
19.	Rutherford B. Hayes	1877–1881	Republican
20.	James A. Garfield	1881	Republican
21.	Chester A. Arthur	1881–1885	Republican
22.	Grover Cleveland	1885–1889	Democrat
23.	Benjamin Harrison	1889–1893	Republican
24.	Grover Cleveland	1893–1897	Democrat
25.	William McKinley	1897–1901	Republican
26.	Theodore Roosevelt	1901–1909	Republican
27.	William Howard Taft	1909–1913	Republican
28.	Woodrow Wilson	1913–1921	Democrat
29.	Warren G. Harding	1921–1923	Republican
30.	Calvin Coolidge	1923–1929	Republican
31.	Herbert Hoover	1929–1933	Republican
32.	Franklin D. Roosevelt	1933–1945	Democrat
33.	Harry S. Truman	1945–1953	Democrat
34.	Dwight D. Eisenhower	1953–1961	Republican
35.	John F. Kennedy	1961–1963	Democrat
36.	Lyndon B. Johnson	1963–1969	Democrat
37.	Richard M. Nixon	1969–1974	Republican
38.	Gerald R. Ford	1974–1977	Republican
39.	Jimmy Carter	1977–1981	Democrat
40.	Ronald W. Reagan	1981–1989	Republican
41.	George Bush	1989–1993	Republican
42.	William Jefferson Clinton	1993–2001	Democrat
43.	George W. Bush	2001–	Republican

Contents

Inventions

An invention is something new and useful that someone has created. It may be a device or a process, simple or complicated, but unique in that it has never been done before. Anyone can be an inventor. You don't need to be a certain age or hold a certain degree. All you need is a new idea.

In this report, students will use items in an inventor's bag that you have prepared to create an extraordinary flying machine. When they are finished, you have everything you need to put on an Invention Convention!

Easy File Folder Reports • EMC 6001 • ©2004 by Evan-Moor Corp.

Before Assigning the Report

1. Prepare the following materials for each student:

   - student direction sheets on pages 88 and 89

   - report reproducibles on pages 90–92

   - a completed Inventor's Bag for each student. The bags and the contents of each bag must be identical. Construction items might include: paper clips, length of string, straws, scrap paper, paper cup, rubber bands, craft sticks, foam chips, and index cards.

     Fold the tops closed and staple on the instructions found on page 93.

2. Decide how to assign the reports. (See the directions on page 2.)

Completing the Report

1. Distribute materials to students.

2. Introduce the report following the guidelines and suggestions on page 2.

3. Explain that each student will create his or her own flying machine from the entire contents of the Inventor's Bag (plus bag and note). Discuss the rules on the note. Be sure to answer all questions at this time.

4. Follow the guidelines on page 3 for assisting students as they work on and complete the report. You may wish to allow time in class to construct the flying machines or assign the project as homework. Creating the flying machines at home adds an element of surprise.

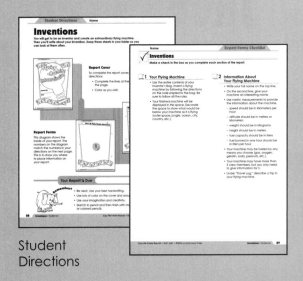

Student Directions

Report Reproducibles

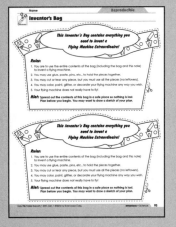

Inventor's Bag Reproducible

Inventions

You will get to be an inventor and create an extraordinary flying machine. Then you'll write about your invention. Keep these sheets in your folder so you can look at them often.

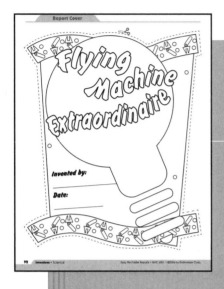

Report Cover

To complete the report cover, follow these directions:

- Complete the lines at the bottom of the page.
- Color as you wish.

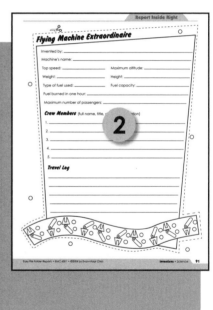

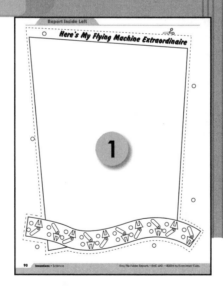

Report Forms

This diagram shows the inside of your report. The numbers on the diagram match the numbers in your directions on the next page. This is to show you where to place information on your report.

Your Report Is Due

Remember!

- Be neat. Use your best handwriting.
- Use lots of color on the cover and around the borders.
- Use your imagination and creativity.
- Sketch in pencil and then finish with markers, crayons, or colored pencils.

Inventions

Make a check in the box as you complete each section of the report.

1 Your Flying Machine

- Use the entire contents of your Inventor's Bag. Invent a flying machine by following the directions on the note stapled to the bag. Be sure to follow all the rules.

- Your finished machine will be displayed in this space. Decorate the space to show what would be below your machine as it is flying (outer space, jungle, ocean, city, country, etc.).

2 Information About Your Flying Machine

- Write your full name on the top line.

- On the second line, give your machine an interesting name.

- Use metric measurements to provide the information about the machine.
  - speed should be in kilometers per hour
  - altitude should be in meters or kilometers
  - weight should be in kilograms
  - height should be in meters
  - fuel capacity should be in liters
  - fuel burned in one hour should be in liters per hour

- Your machine may be fueled by any means you choose (gas, oxygen, gelatin, soda, peanuts, etc.).

- Your machine may have more than 5 crew members, but you only need to give information for 5.

- Under "Travel Log," describe a trip in your flying machine.

Here's My Flying Machine Extraordinaire

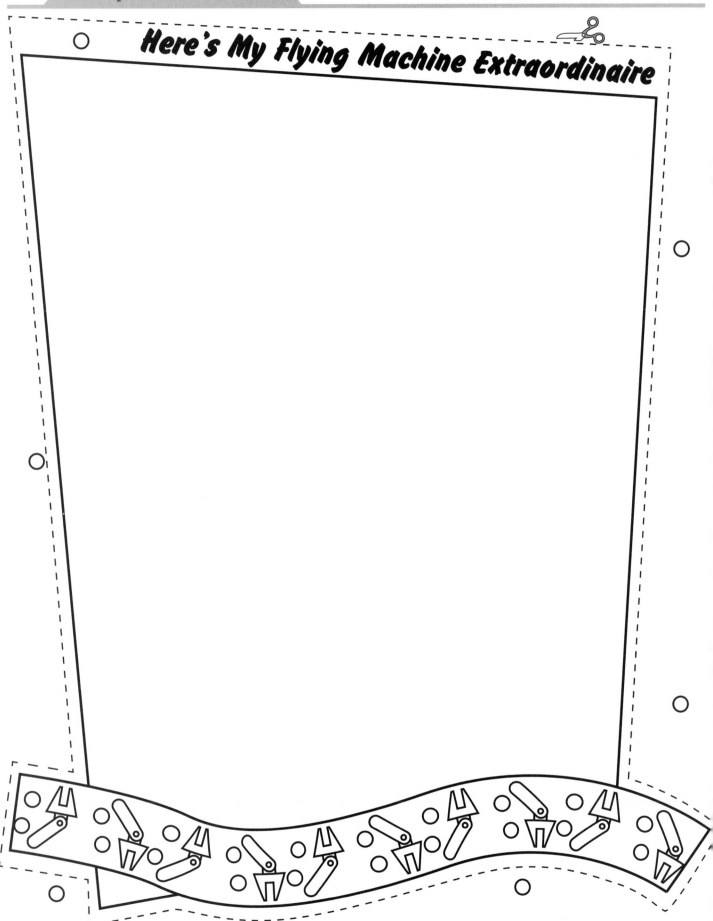

Easy File Folder Reports • EMC 6001 • ©2004 by Evan-Moor Corp.

Flying Machine Extraordinaire

Invented by: _____

Machine's name: _____

Top speed: _____ Maximum altitude: _____

Weight: _____ Height: _____

Type of fuel used: _____ Fuel capacity: _____

Fuel burned in one hour: _____

Maximum number of passengers: _____

Crew Members (full name, title, and job description)

1. _____

2. _____

3. _____

4. _____

5. _____

Travel Log

_____

_____

_____

_____

_____

_____

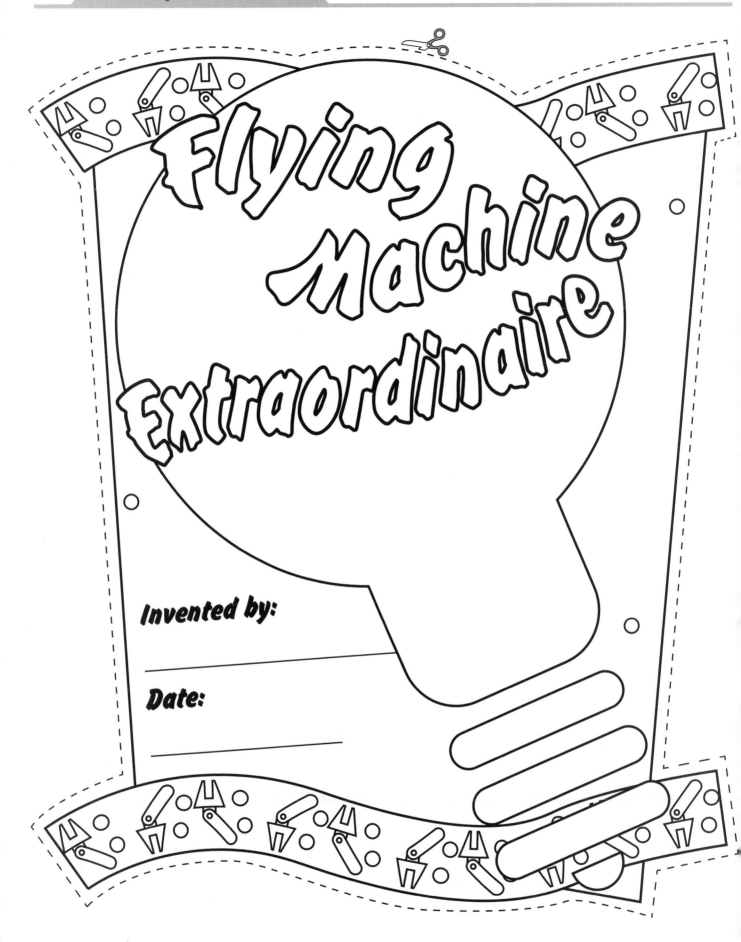

Flying Machine Extraordinaire

Invented by:

_____

Date:

_____

Easy File Folder Reports • EMC 6001 • ©2004 by Evan-Moor Corp.

Inventor's Bag

This Inventor's Bag contains everything you need to invent a Flying Machine Extraordinaire!

Rules:

1. You are to use the entire contents of the bag (including the bag and this note) to invent a flying machine.

2. You may use glue, paste, pins, etc., to hold the pieces together.

3. You may cut or tear any piece, but you must use all the pieces (no leftovers).

4. You may color, paint, glitter, or decorate your flying machine any way you wish.

5. Your flying machine does not really have to fly!

Hint: Spread out the contents of this bag in a safe place so nothing is lost. Plan before you begin. You may want to draw a sketch of your plan.

This Inventor's Bag contains everything you need to invent a Flying Machine Extraordinaire!

Rules:

1. You are to use the entire contents of the bag (including the bag and this note) to invent a flying machine.

2. You may use glue, paste, pins, etc., to hold the pieces together.

3. You may cut or tear any piece, but you must use all the pieces (no leftovers).

4. You may color, paint, glitter, or decorate your flying machine any way you wish.

5. Your flying machine does not really have to fly!

Hint: Spread out the contents of this bag in a safe place so nothing is lost. Plan before you begin. You may want to draw a sketch of your plan.

National Parks

Congress laid the foundation of the U.S. National Park System in 1872 by establishing Yellowstone National Park. Today, the National Park System comprises nearly 400 areas totaling almost 79 million acres. In this report, each student will have a chance to study one specific park. For some students, learning about the beauty our National Parks offer may be the beginning of a lifelong commitment to the maintenance of our fragile ecosystems.

Before Assigning the Report

1. Prepare the following materials for each student:

   - student direction sheets on pages 96 and 97

   - report reproducibles on pages 98–100

   - file folder, cut to size for stand-up visual (See page 6.)

   - assorted colors of construction paper

   - foil star

   - index cards or paper for note-taking

2. Decide how to assign the reports. (See the directions on page 2 and the list of National Parks on page 101.)

Completing the Report

1. Distribute materials to students.

2. Introduce the report following the guidelines and suggestions on page 2.

3. Follow the guidelines on page 3 for assisting students as they work on and complete the report.

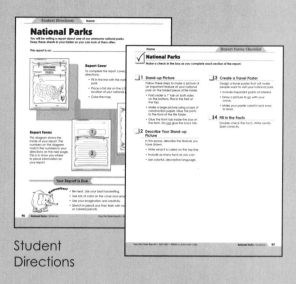

Student Directions

Report Reproducibles

National Parks Reproducible

National Parks

You will be writing a report about one of our awesome national parks.
Keep these sheets in your folder so you can look at them often.

This report is on: _____

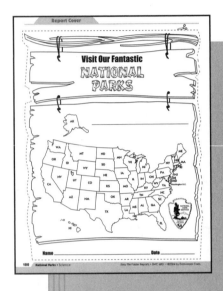

Report Cover

To complete the report cover, follow these directions:

- Fill in the top line with the name of your national park.
- Place a foil star on the U.S. map to show the location of your national park.
- Color the map.

Report Forms

This diagram shows the inside of your report. The numbers on the diagram match the numbers in your directions on the next page. This is to show you where to place information on your report.

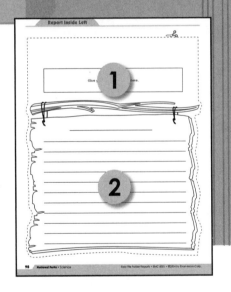

Your Report Is Due

Remember!

- Be neat. Use your best handwriting.
- Use lots of color on the cover and around the borders.
- Use your imagination and creativity.
- Sketch in pencil and then finish with markers, crayons, or colored pencils.

National Parks

Make a check in the box as you complete each section of the report.

1 Stand-up Picture

Follow these steps to make a picture of an important feature of your national park on the folded piece of file folder.

- Fold under a 1" (2.5 cm) tab on both sides on the bottom. Place the fold at the top.

- Make a large picture using scraps of construction paper. Glue the parts to the front of the file folder.

- Glue the front tab inside the box on the form. Do <u>not</u> glue the back tab.

2 Describe Your Stand-up Picture

In this space, describe the feature you have drawn.

- Write what it is called on the top line.

- Include as many facts as you can.

- Use colorful, descriptive language.

3 Create a Travel Poster

Design a travel poster that will make people want to visit your national park.

- Include important points of interest.

- Draw a picture to go with your words.

- Make your poster colorful and easy to read.

4 Fill in the Facts

Double-check the facts. Write neatly. Spell correctly.

Glue your stand-up picture here.

VISIT FANTASTIC

FACTS

Name _____

Location _____

Size _____

NATIONAL
PARK
SERVICE

Department
of the Interior

Visit Our Fantastic
NATIONAL PARKS

Name _____ Date _____

  Easy File Folder Reports • EMC 6001 • ©2004 by Evan-Moor Corp.

National Parks

The East
Acadia
Biscayne
Everglades
Great Smoky Mountains
Hot Springs
Isle Royale
Mammoth Cave
Shenandoah
Virgin Islands
Voyageurs

The Southwest
Big Bend
Carlsbad
Guadalupe

The Colorado Plateau
Arches
Bryce Canyon
Canyonlands
Capitol Reef
Grand Canyon
Great Basin
Mesa Verde
Petrified Forest
Zion

The Pacific Southwest
Channel Islands
Kings Canyon

Hawaii Volcanoes
Haleakala
Sequoia
Yosemite

The Rocky Mountains
Badlands
Glacier
Grand Teton
Rocky Mountain
Theodore Roosevelt
Wind Cave
Yellowstone

The Pacific Northwest
Crater Lake
Lassen Volcanic
Mount Rainier
North Cascades
Olympic
Redwood

Alaska
Denali
Gates of the Arctic
Glacier Bay
Katmai
Kenai Fjords
Kobuk Valley
Lake Clark
Wrangell-St. Elias

Seeds are truly amazing. Within each seed is everything necessary to reproduce the parent plant. In this report, students will record their observations on the sprouting of two different seeds. Allow time for lengthy observations and discussion of growth patterns observed. Let students decide what to do with their seeds after the reports have been displayed.

From Seed to Plant

Before Assigning the Report

1. Prepare the following materials for each student:

   - student direction sheets on pages 104 and 105

   - report reproducibles on pages 106–108

   - observation form on page 109—several per student, depending on the anticipated length of the observation period

   - 2 clear plastic cups

   - cotton to line cups (use cotton rolls); cut the cotton in correctly sized strips and dampen the strips just before distributing them.

   - two large, quick-sprouting seeds (bean, nasturtium, pumpkin, for example)

   - a permanent black marker

   - source for water

   - rulers to measure plant growth

2. Decide on an area where seed cups can be placed during the observation period.

3. Decide how to assign the reports. (See the directions on page 2.)

4. Decide how students will access the information needed to label the drawings on the cover of their reports. Suggestions:

   - Make an overhead transparency of page 108 and guide students in labeling the parts of the seed and plant.

   - Provide science reference materials that contain labeled plant drawings.

   - Allow students to use appropriate online reference sources that you have bookmarked.

Completing the Report

1. Distribute materials to students. Write the names of the seeds on the chalkboard so that students can label their cups.

2. Introduce the report following the guidelines and suggestions on page 2.

3. Follow the guidelines on page 3 for assisting students as they work on and complete the report.

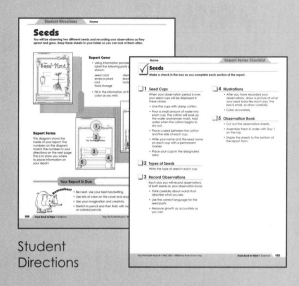

Student Directions

Report Reproducibles

Seeds

You will be observing two different seeds and recording your observations as they sprout and grow. Keep these sheets in your folder so you can look at them often.

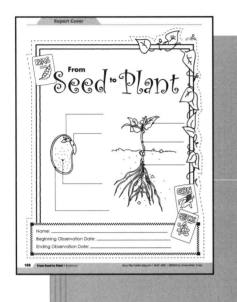

Report Cover

- Using information provided by your teacher, label the following parts of the seed and plant shown:

  seed coat   stem
  embryo plant   leaves
  root   roots
  food storage

- Fill in the information at the bottom, and then color as you wish.

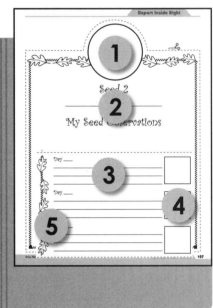

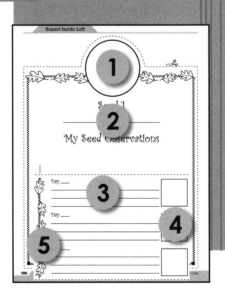

Report Forms

This diagram shows the inside of your report. The numbers on the diagram match the numbers in your directions on the next page. This is to show you where to place information on your report.

Your Report Is Due

Remember!

- Be neat. Use your best handwriting.
- Use lots of color on the cover and around the borders.
- Use your imagination and creativity.
- Sketch in pencil and then finish with markers, crayons, or colored pencils.

Seeds

Make a check in the box as you complete each section of the report.

☐ 1 Seed Cups

When your observation period is over, your seed cups will be displayed in these circles.

- Line the cups with damp cotton.

- Pour a small amount of water into each cup. The cotton will soak up the water and remain moist. Add water when the cotton begins to dry out.

- Place a seed between the cotton and the side of each cup.

- Write your name and the seed name on each cup with a permanent marker.

- Place your cups in the designated area.

☐ 2 Types of Seeds

Write the type of seed in each cup.

☐ 3 Record Observations

Each day you will record observations of both seeds on your observation sheets.

- Think carefully about words that describe what you see.

- Use the correct language for the seed parts.

- Measure growth as accurately as you can.

☐ 4 Illustrations

- After you have recorded your observations, draw a picture of what your seed looks like each day. The box is small, so draw carefully.

- Color accurately.

☐ 5 Observation Book

- Cut out the observation sheets.

- Assemble them in order with Day 1 on the top.

- Staple the sheets to the bottom of the report form.

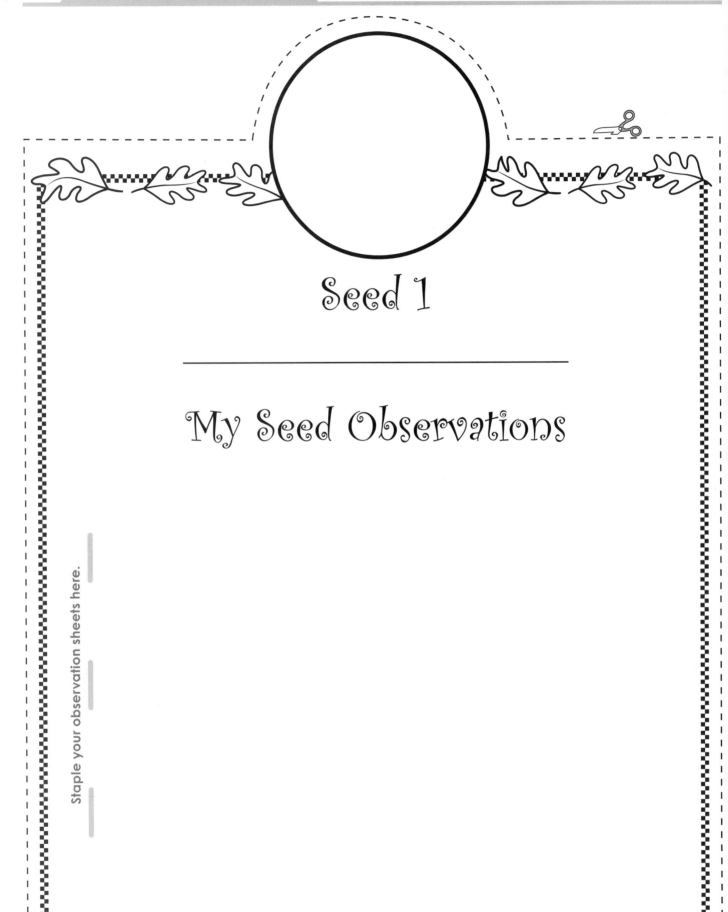

Seed 1

My Seed Observations

Staple your observation sheets here.

Seed 2

_____

My Seed Observations

Staple your observation sheets here.

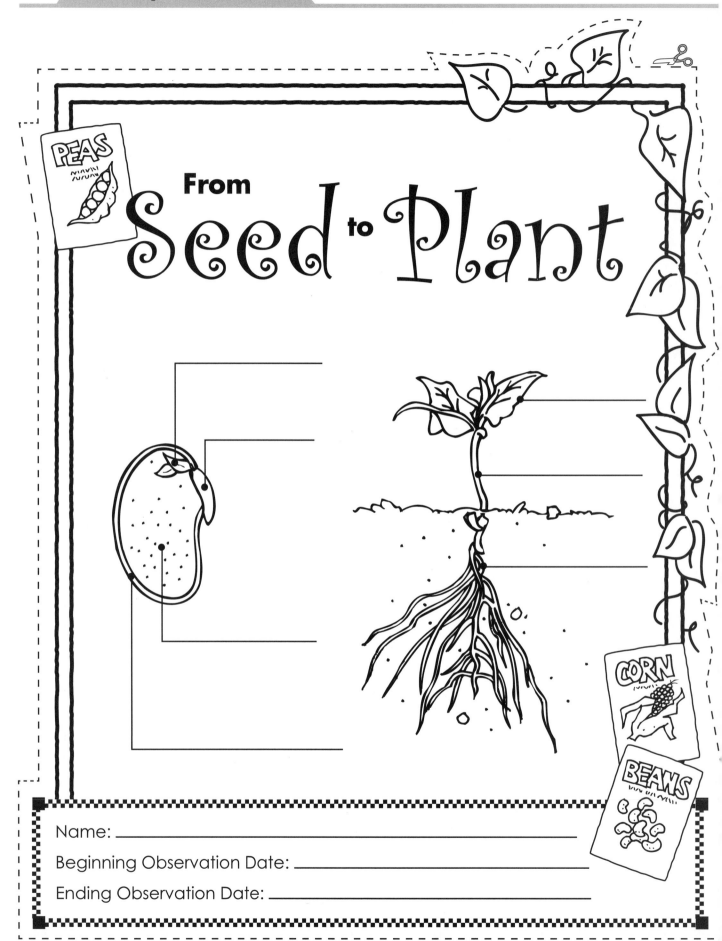

From
Seed to Plant

Name: _____

Beginning Observation Date: _____

Ending Observation Date: _____

 Easy File Folder Reports • EMC 6001 • ©2004 by Evan-Moor Corp.

Observation Sheet

Day ____

Day ____

Day ____

Day ____

Day ____

Day ____

Desert Dwellers

There are about 20 major deserts in the world, spread out on five continents. They cover almost 15% of the Earth's land area—about the size of South America. A desert is a place that has very little vegetation, receives less than 10 inches (25 cm) of rain each year, and has a high rate of evaporation. Most of the world's deserts are hot deserts. However, some, such as the Gobi Desert in Mongolia, are cold.

Many people think that the desert has as little life as it has rainfall, but this is not true. The desert is alive with many amazing plants and animals. Students are to report on one desert dweller, studying its adaptations for survival. They may learn to view deserts not as being "deserted," but as being abundantly full.

Before Assigning the Report

1. Prepare the following materials for each student:

   - student direction sheets on pages 112 and 113

   - report reproducibles on pages 114–116

   - file folder, cut to size for stand-up visual (See page 6.)

   - access to an assortment of craft materials and construction paper scraps

   - 6 sheets of plain paper, cut 4" x 7" (10 x 18 cm) for answering questions

   - index cards for note-taking

2. Decide how to assign the reports. (See the directions on page 2 and the list of desert plants and animals on page 117.) You may need to limit the list, depending on availability of information sources.

Completing the Report

1. Distribute materials to students.

2. Introduce the report following the guidelines and suggestions on page 2.

3. Follow the guidelines on page 3 for assisting students as they work on and complete the report. You may wish to provide the answers to item 3, labeling deserts on the world map. Or assign each student to find the location of one of the nine deserts listed on page 117 and compile the answers as a class. Label other deserts if desired.

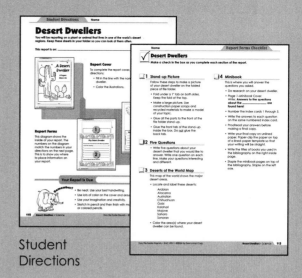

Student Directions

Report Reproducibles

Desert Plants & Animals Reproducible

Desert Dwellers

You will be reporting on a plant or animal that lives in one of the world's desert regions. Keep these sheets in your folder so you can look at them often.

This report is on: _____

Report Cover

To complete the report cover, follow these directions:

- Fill in the line with the name of your desert dweller.
- Color the illustrations.

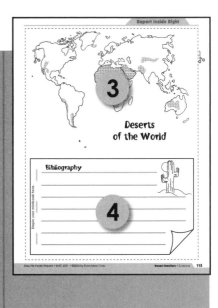

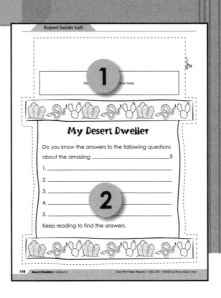

Report Forms

This diagram shows the inside of your report. The numbers on the diagram match the numbers in your directions on the next page. This is to show you where to place information on your report.

Your Report Is Due

Remember!

- Be neat. Use your best handwriting.
- Use lots of color on the cover and around the borders.
- Use your imagination and creativity.
- Sketch in pencil and then finish with markers, crayons, or colored pencils.

Desert Dwellers

Make a check in the box as you complete each section of the report.

1 Stand-up Picture

Follow these steps to make a picture of your desert dweller on the folded piece of file folder.

- Fold under a 1" (2.5 cm) tab on both sides. Keep the fold at the top.

- Make a large picture. Use construction paper scraps and recycled materials to make a model of your topic.

- Glue all the parts to the front of the file folder stand-up.

- Glue the front tab of the stand-up inside the box. Do <u>not</u> glue the back tab.

2 Five Questions

- Write five questions about your desert dweller that you would like to answer. Write one question on each line. Make your questions interesting and different.

3 Deserts of the World Map

This map of the world shows the major desert areas.

- Locate and label these deserts:

  Arabian
  Atacama
  Australian
  Chihuahuan
  Gobi
  Kalahari
  Mojave
  Sahara
  Sonoran

- Color the area(s) where your desert dweller can be found.

4 Minibook

This is where you will answer the questions you asked.

- Do research on your desert dweller.

- *Page 1–Minibook Cover.*
  Write: **Answers to the questions about the _____ are found here!**

- Number the index cards 1 through 5.

- Write the answers to each question on the same numbered index card.

- Proofread your answers before making a final copy.

- Write your final copy on unlined paper. Paper-clip the paper on top of a lined-paper template so that your writing will be straight.

- Write the titles of books you used in the bibliography on the right inside page.

- Staple the minibook pages on top of the bibliography. Staple on the left side.

Glue your stand-up picture here.

My Desert Dweller

Do you know the answers to the following questions about the amazing _____?

1. _____

2. _____

3. _____

4. _____

5. _____

Keep reading to find the answers.

 Easy File Folder Reports • EMC 6001 • ©2004 by Evan-Moor Corp.

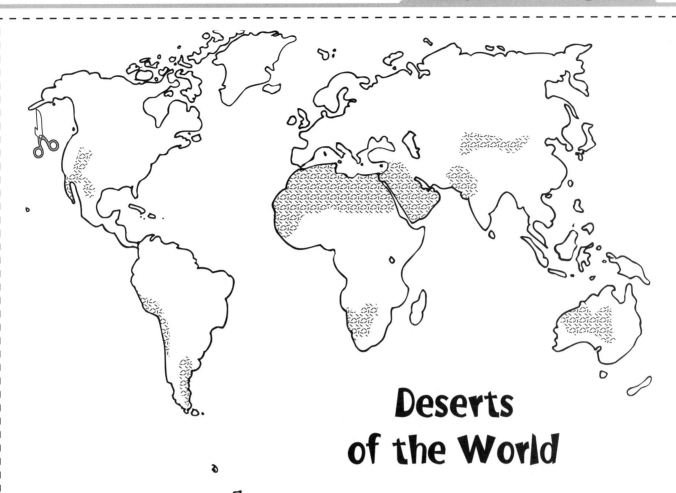

Deserts of the World

Staple your minibook here.

Bibliography

_____

_____

_____

_____

_____

_____

A Desert Dweller

A Report About the

_____

Name: _____   Date: _____

   Easy File Folder Reports • EMC 6001 • ©2004 by Evan-Moor Corp.

Desert Plants & Animals

Name of Desert	Location	Plants	Animals	
Arabian	Arabian Peninsula	acacia oleander	dromedary camel gazelle	jackal oryx
Atacama	coasts of Chile & Peru	cardon cactus tamaruga trees	llama Peruvian Fox	
Australian	Australia	casuarina tree eucalyptus saltbush	dingo kangaroo thorny devil	rabbit-eared bandicoot

Chihuahaun	north & central Mexico; parts of Arizona, New Mexico, & Texas	creosote bush
		mesquite
		barrel cactus
		teddy bear cholla
		prickly pear cactus
			coyote
			diamondback
			  rattlesnake
			javalina
				roadrunner
				western spade-
				  foot toad
				mule deer

Gobi	northern China & southern Mongolia	camel's thorn	Bactrian camel gazelle gerbil	jerboa wolf
Kalahari	southwestern Africa	baobob tree	hyena jackal springbok	
Mojave	California, Nevada, Arizona	creosote bush sand verbena Joshua tree	bighorn sheep chuckwalla coyote jackrabbit	sidewinder kit fox mule deer desert iguana
Sahara	northern Africa	acacia tamarisks	fennec fox horned viper addax antelope dorcas gazelle	jerboa jackal spiny-tailed lizard
Sonoran	Arizona, California, Baja California	agave ocotillo mesquite paloverde saguaro creosote bush barrel cactus teddy bear cholla prickly pear cactus smoke tree	coati elf owl Gila monster kangaroo rat sidewinder pack rat roadrunner	tarantula desert tortoise kit fox mule deer desert iguana scorpion

Forests cover nearly one-third of the continental United States. Forests provide us with many products and places for recreation and are very important in protecting our soil and water supplies.

More than 700 different kinds of trees are found in the U.S. forests. But forests are not just trees. Forests are complex ecosystems of plants, animals, water, and soil. Wildlife can be found in all layers of the forest—from the canopy down to the forest floor.

In this report, students will choose a forest creature to study. In the course of their studies, they may gain an appreciation for the complex relationships of animals and plants.

Forest Creatures

Before Assigning the Report

1. Prepare the following materials for each student:
   - student direction sheets on pages 120 and 121
   - report reproducibles on pages 122–124
   - 6" x 12" (15 x 30.5 cm) white drawing paper for the pop-up
   - 6" x 12" (15 x 30.5 cm) construction paper for the pop-up folder cover
   - scraps of construction paper in various colors and sizes
   - 6 sheets of plain paper, cut 4" x 7" (10 x 18 cm)
   - index cards for note-taking

2. Decide how to assign the reports. (See the directions on page 2 and the list of forest animals on page 125.)

3. Gather sources from which students can take colored photographs of their forest creatures—old nature magazines and student newspapers, bookmarked Internet sites, etc.

Completing the Report

1. Distribute materials to students.

2. Introduce the report following the guidelines and suggestions on page 2.

3. Follow the guidelines on page 3 for assisting students as they work on and complete the report.

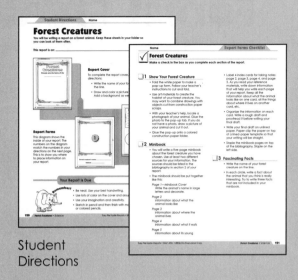

Student Directions

Report Reproducibles

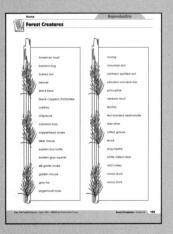

Forest Creatures Reproducible

Forest Creatures

You will be writing a report on a forest animal. Keep these sheets in your folder so you can look at them often.

This report is on: _____

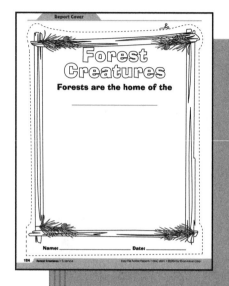

Report Cover

To complete the report cover, follow these directions:

- Write the name of your forest creature on the top line.
- Draw and color a picture of the animal. Add a background as well.

Report Forms

This diagram shows the inside of your report. The numbers on the diagram match the numbers in your directions on the next page. This is to show you where to place information on your report.

Your Report Is Due ( )

Remember!

- Be neat. Use your best handwriting.
- Use lots of color on the cover and around the borders.
- Use your imagination and creativity.
- Sketch in pencil and then finish with markers, crayons, or colored pencils.

Forest Creatures

Make a check in the box as you complete each section of the report.

☐ 1 Show Your Forest Creature

- Fold the white paper to make a pop-up form. Follow your teacher's instructions to cut and fold.

- Use art materials to create the habitat of your forest creature. You may want to combine drawings with objects cut from construction paper scraps.

- With your teacher's help, locate a photograph of your animal. Glue the photo to the pop-up tab. If you do not have a photo, draw a picture of your animal and cut it out.

- Glue the pop-up onto a colored construction paper folder.

☐ 2 Minibook

- You will write a five-page minibook about the forest creature you have chosen. Use at least two different sources for your information. The sources should be listed in the bibliography in section 2 of your report.

- The minibook should be put together like this:

  Page 1—Minibook Cover
  Write the animal's name in large letters and decorate.

  Page 2
  information about what the animal looks like

  Page 3
  information about where the animal lives

  Page 4
  information about what it eats

  Page 5
  information about its young

- Label 4 index cards for taking notes: page 2, page 3, page 4, and page 5. As you read your reference materials, write down information that will help you write each page of your report. Keep all the information about what the animal looks like on one card, all the things about where it lives on another card, etc.

- Organize the information on each card. Write a rough draft and proofread it before writing your final draft.

- Write your final draft on unlined paper. Paper-clip the paper on top of a lined-paper template so that your writing will be straight.

- Staple the minibook pages on top of the bibliography. Staple on the left side.

☐ 3 Fascinating Facts

- Write the name of your forest creature on the line.

- In each circle, write a fact about the animal that you think is really interesting. Try to write three facts that are not included in your minibook.

Forest creature's name: _____

Habitat: _____

     Easy File Folder Reports • EMC 6001 • ©2004 by Evan-Moor Corp.

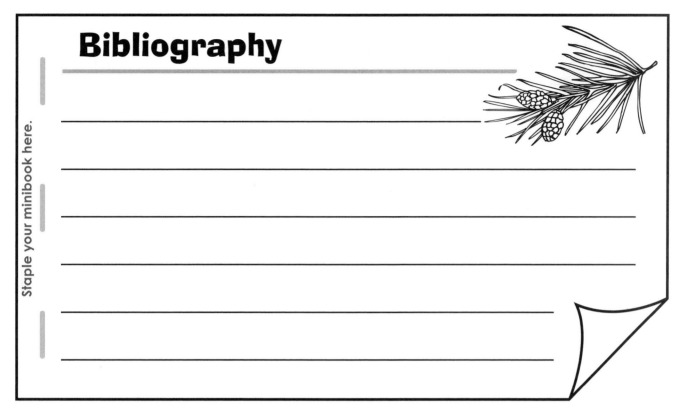

Bibliography

Staple your minibook here.

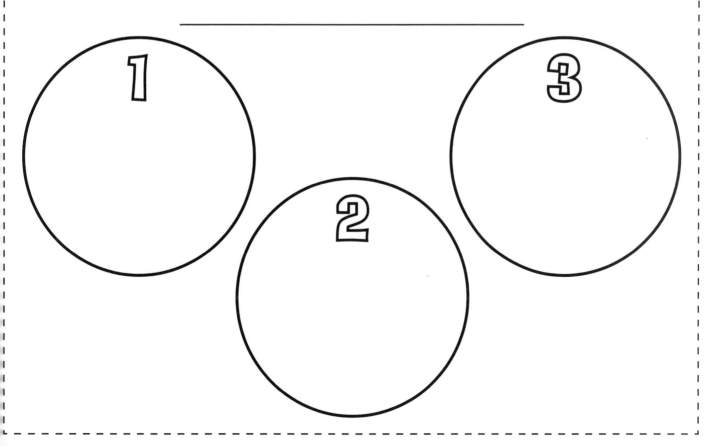

3 **super-duper facts about the**

1

2

3

Forest Creatures

Forests are the home of the

_____

Name: _____ **Date:** _____

 Easy File Folder Reports • EMC 6001 • ©2004 by Evan-Moor Corp.

Forest Creatures

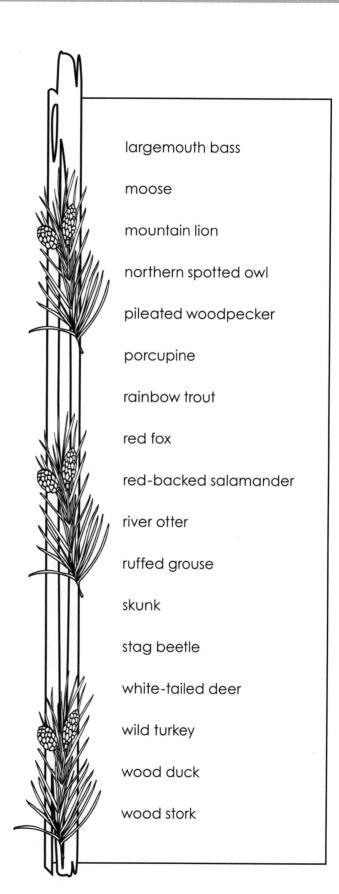

American toad

banana slug

barred owl

beaver

black bear

black-capped chickadee

caribou

chipmunk

common loon

copperhead snake

deer mouse

eastern box turtle

eastern gray squirrel

elk

garter snake

golden mouse

gray fox

largemouth bass

moose

mountain lion

northern spotted owl

pileated woodpecker

porcupine

rainbow trout

red fox

red-backed salamander

river otter

ruffed grouse

skunk

stag beetle

white-tailed deer

wild turkey

wood duck

wood stork

Minerals

Minerals are the most common solid materials found on Earth. There are about 3,000 kinds of minerals. Minerals include common substances such as rock salt and pencil "lead," and rare ones such as gold and silver.

A substance is a mineral if it has all of these four features:

- It is found in nature.

- It has the same chemical makeup wherever it is found. For example, sand is not a mineral because sand from different places can have different chemical makeups.

- Its atoms form solid units called crystals.

- It is made up of substances that were never alive. Coal, petroleum, and natural gas are not minerals partly because they were formed from fossilized animals and plants.

In this report, students will examine a particular mineral, look at its properties, and examine its uses.

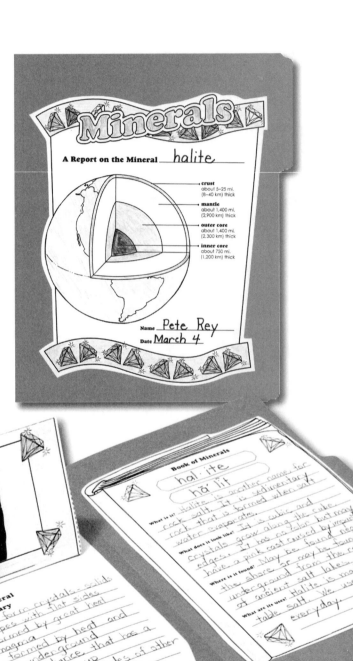

Easy File Folder Reports • EMC 6001 • ©2004 by Evan-Moor Corp.

Before Assigning the Report

1. Prepare the following materials for each student:

   - student direction sheets on pages 128 and 129
   - report reproducibles on pages 130–133
   - bookmarked Internet sites on minerals

2. Decide how to assign the reports. (See the directions on page 2 and the list of minerals on page 133.) As students are not likely to be familiar with many of the minerals listed, it is probably best to assign each student a mineral.

3. Gather photos of the minerals on the list or plan how students will locate a photo of their minerals. There are several excellent Web sites that have photos that can be printed. Search for "minerals."

Completing the Report

1. Distribute materials to students.

2. Introduce the report following the guidelines and suggestions on page 2.

3. Follow the guidelines on page 3 for assisting students as they work on and complete the report. This report is especially appropriate for using Internet sources or online and CD-ROM encyclopedias.

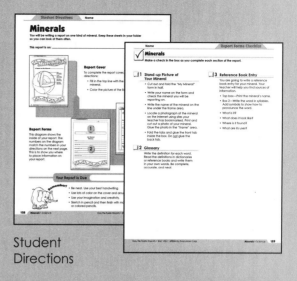

Student Directions

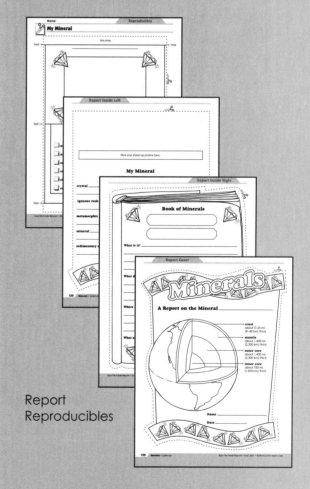

Report Reproducibles

Minerals

You will be writing a report on one kind of mineral. Keep these sheets in your folder so you can look at them often.

This report is on: _____

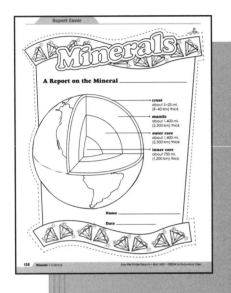

Report Cover

To complete the report cover, follow these directions:

- Fill in the top line with the name of your mineral.
- Color the picture of the Earth and the border.

Report Forms

This diagram shows the inside of your report. The numbers on the diagram match the numbers in your directions on the next page. This is to show you where to place information on your report.

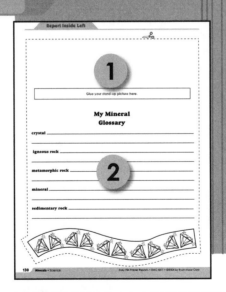

Your Report Is Due

Remember!

- Be neat. Use your best handwriting.
- Use lots of color on the cover and around the borders.
- Use your imagination and creativity.
- Sketch in pencil and then finish with markers, crayons, or colored pencils.

Minerals

Make a check in the box as you complete each section of the report.

1 Stand-up Picture of Your Mineral

- Cut out and fold the "My Mineral" form in half.

- Write your name on the form and check the mineral you will be reporting on.

- Write the name of the mineral on the line under the frame area.

- Locate a photograph of the mineral on the Internet using sites your teacher has bookmarked. Print and cut out a photo of your mineral. Glue the photo in the "frame" area.

- Fold the tabs and glue the front tab inside the box. Do <u>not</u> glue the back tab.

2 Glossary

Write the definition for each word. Read the definitions in dictionaries or reference books and write them in your own words. Be complete, accurate, and neat.

3 Reference Book Entry

You are going to write a reference book entry for your mineral. Your teacher will help you find sources of information.

- Top box—Print the mineral's name.

- Box 2—Write the word in syllables. Add symbols to show how to pronounce the word.

- What is it?

- What does it look like?

- Where is it found?

- What are its uses?

Glue your stand-up picture here.

My Mineral Glossary

crystal _____

_____

igneous rock _____

_____

metamorphic rock _____

_____

mineral _____

_____

sedimentary rock _____

_____

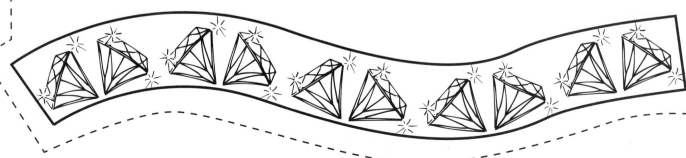

Book of Minerals

What is it? _____

_____

_____

_____

What does it look like? _____

_____

_____

_____

_____

Where is it found? _____

_____

_____

_____

_____

What are its uses? _____

_____

_____

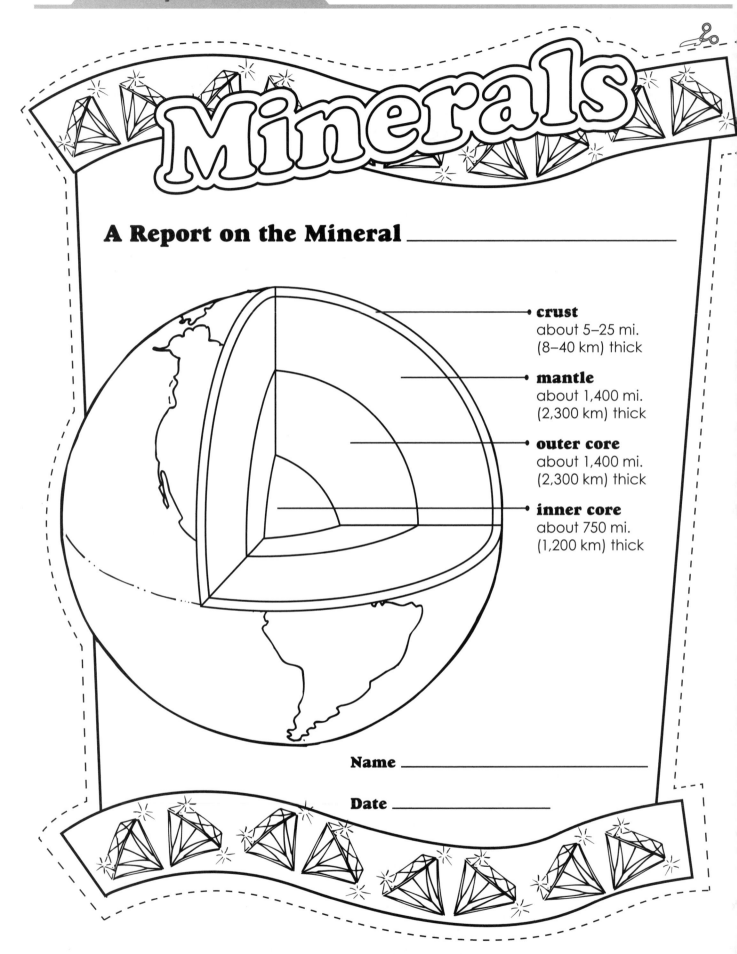

Minerals

A Report on the Mineral _____

- **crust**
  about 5–25 mi.
  (8–40 km) thick

- **mantle**
  about 1,400 mi.
  (2,300 km) thick

- **outer core**
  about 1,400 mi.
  (2,300 km) thick

- **inner core**
  about 750 mi.
  (1,200 km) thick

Name _____

Date _____

   Easy File Folder Reports • EMC 6001 • ©2004 by Evan-Moor Corp.

My Mineral

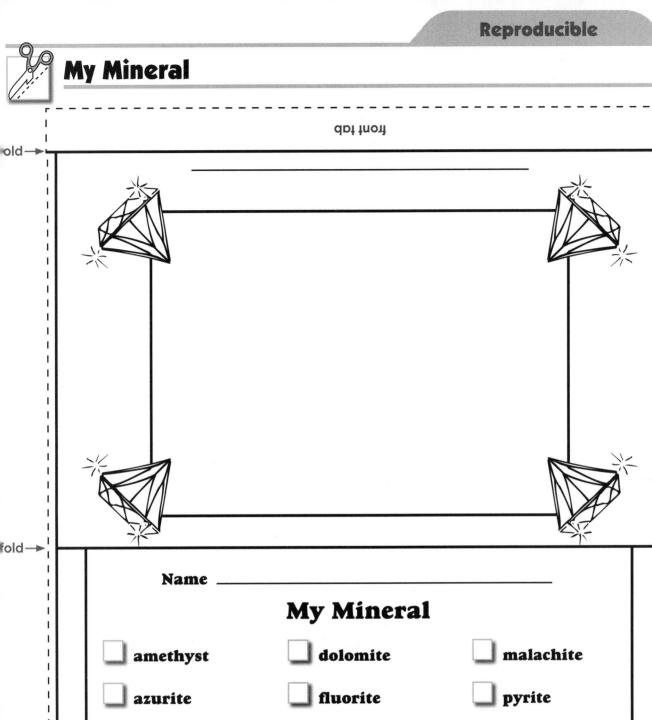

front tab

Name _____

My Mineral

- ☐ amethyst
- ☐ azurite
- ☐ emerald
- ☐ carnelian
- ☐ cinnabar
- ☐ corundum

- ☐ dolomite
- ☐ fluorite
- ☐ garnet
- ☐ halite
- ☐ hermatite
- ☐ jasper

- ☐ malachite
- ☐ pyrite
- ☐ quartz
- ☐ sulphur
- ☐ talc
- ☐ _____

back tab

With over 70% of our planet covered with water, it is important that students develop an understanding of this liquid environment and the creatures that live in it. Both students who live near the ocean and those who don't will be fascinated to learn about strange creatures that never see light, or underwater mountains taller than Mount Everest.

Use this report in conjunction with a visit to an aquarium or as a component of a science unit. As students learn about the treasures of the ocean, they will be more likely to realize the importance of protecting this vital environment.

Life in the Ocean

Easy File Folder Reports • EMC 6001 • ©2004 by Evan-Moor Corp.

Before Assigning the Report

1. Prepare the following materials for each student:

   - student direction sheets on pages 136 and 137
   - report reproducibles on pages 138–141
   - 6" x 8" (15 x 20 cm) colored construction paper, for pop-up folder cover
   - paper for drawing sea creatures for pop-up page
   - 6 sheets of plain paper, cut 4" x 7" (10 x 18 cm), for minibook
   - index cards for note-taking

2. Decide how to assign the reports. (See the directions on page 2 and the list of marine animals on page 142).

Completing the Report

1. Distribute materials to students.

2. Introduce the report following the guidelines and suggestions on page 2.

3. Explain to students that they will be using first person voice in writing this report. They will be writing as if they were the marine animals being reported on. Model how to write the minibook in first person.

4. Directions for making pop-ups are on page 8. After students have had time to research their animal, you may wish to do the pop-up page together.

5. Follow the guidelines on page 3 for assisting students as they work on and complete the report.

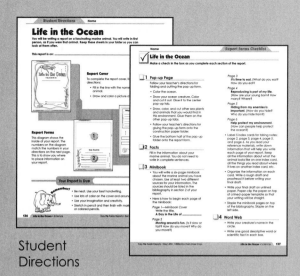

Student Directions

Report Reproducibles

Life in the Ocean Reproducible

Life in the Ocean

You will be writing a report on a fascinating marine animal. You will write in first person, as if you were that animal. Keep these sheets in your folder so you can look at them often.

This report is on: _____

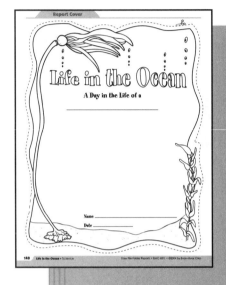

Report Cover

To complete the report cover, follow these directions:

- Fill in the line with the name of your marine animal.
- Draw and color a picture of the animal.

Report Forms

This diagram shows the inside of your report. The numbers on the diagram match the numbers in your directions on the next page. This is to show you where to place information on your report.

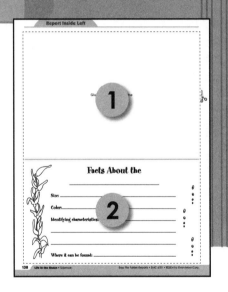

Your Report Is Due

Remember!

- Be neat. Use your best handwriting.
- Use lots of color on the cover and around the borders.
- Use your imagination and creativity.
- Sketch in pencil and then finish with markers, crayons, or colored pencils.

Life in the Ocean

Make a check in the box as you complete each section of the report.

1 Pop-up Page

Follow your teacher's directions for folding and cutting the pop-up form.

- Color the ocean.

- Draw your ocean creature. Color and cut it out. Glue it to the center pop-up tab.

- Draw, color, and cut other sea plants and animals that you would find in this environment. Glue them on the other pop-up tabs.

- Follow your teacher's directions for gluing the pop-up form onto the construction paper folder.

- Glue the bottom half of the pop-up folder onto the report form.

2 Facts

Fill in the information about your marine animal. You do not need to write in complete sentences.

3 Minibook

- You will write a six-page minibook about the marine animal you have chosen. Use at least two different sources for your information. The sources should be listed in the bibliography in section 2 of your report.

- Here is how to begin each page of the minibook:

  Page 1—Minibook Cover
  Write the title,
  A Day in the Life of _____

  Page 2
  Moving around is fun. (Is it slow or fast? How do you move? Why do you move?)

Page 3
It's time to eat. (What do you eat? How do you eat?)

Page 4
Reproducing is part of my life. (How are your young born? How many? Where?)

Page 5
Hiding from my enemies is important. (How do you hide? Who do you hide from?)

Page 6
Help protect my environment. (How can people help protect the ocean?)

- Label 5 index cards for taking notes: page 2, page 3, page 4, page 5, and page 6. As you read your reference materials, write down information that will help you write each page of your report. Keep all the information about what the animal looks like on one index card, all the things you read about where it lives on another index card, etc.

- Organize the information on each card. Write a rough draft and proofread it before writing your final draft.

- Write your final draft on unlined paper. Paper-clip the paper on top of a lined-paper template so that your writing will be straight.

- Staple the minibook pages on top of the bibliography. Staple on the left side.

4 Word Web

- Write your creature's name in the circle.

- Write one good descriptive word or scientific fact in each box.

Glue the bottom half of the
pop-up folder here.

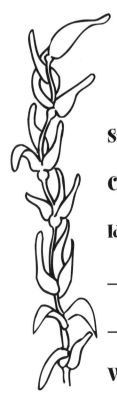

Facts About the

_____

Size: _____

Color:_____

Identifying characteristics: _____

_____

_____

Where it can be found: _____

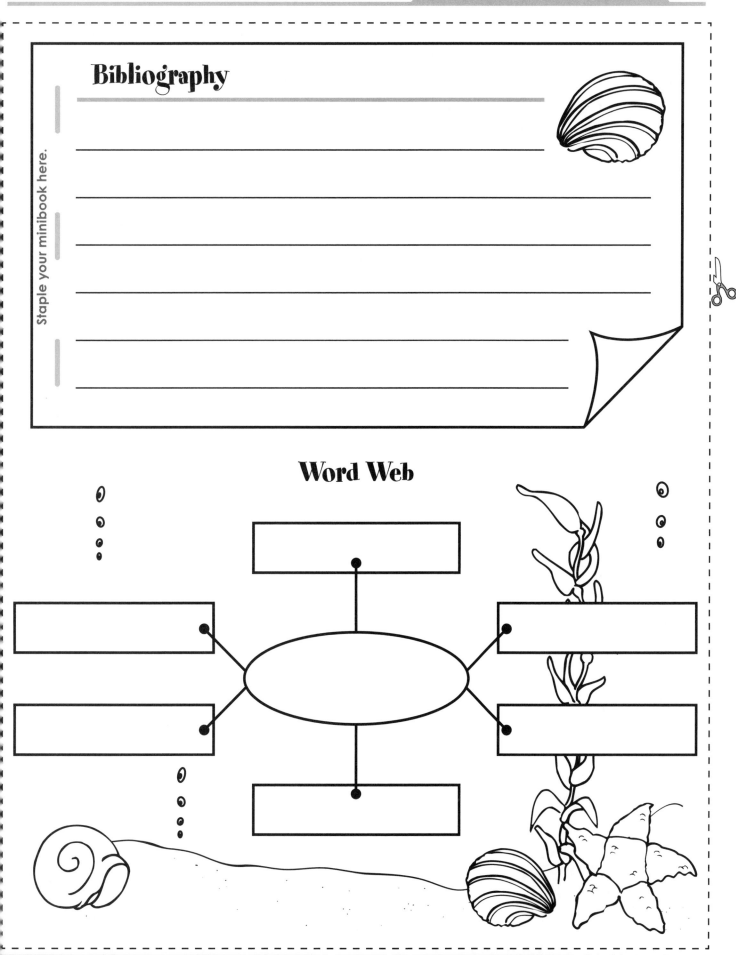

Bibliography

Staple your minibook here.

Word Web

Life in the Ocean

A Day in the Life of a

_____

Name _____

Date _____

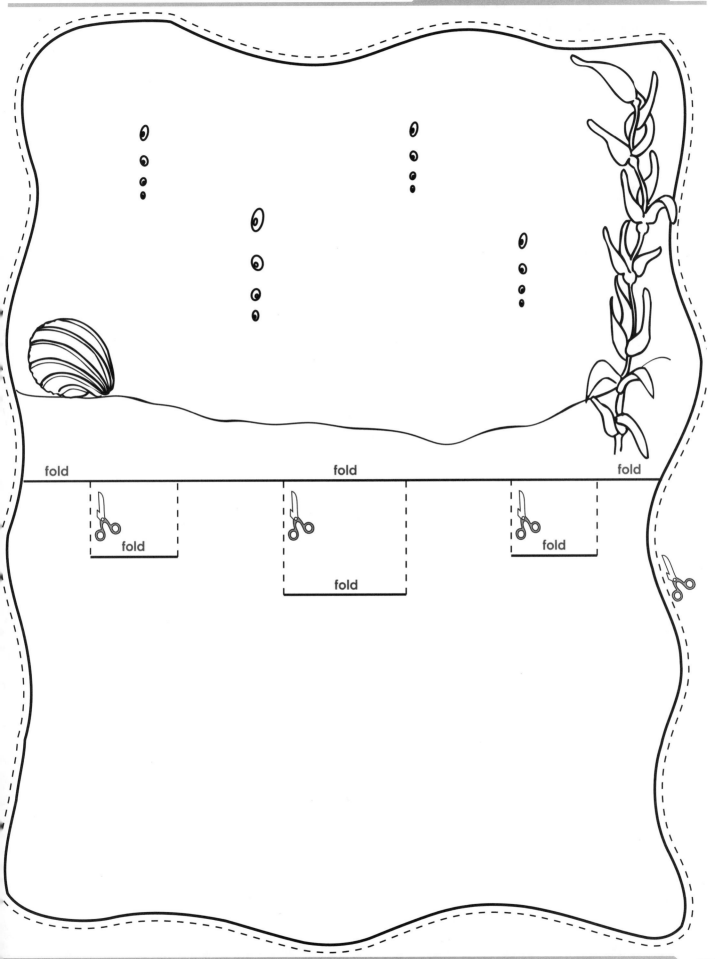

fold   fold   fold

fold   fold

fold

Life in the Ocean

Tidal Zone	barnacle	limpet sea star	sea anemone
	brittle sea star	lugworm	sea horse
	clam	mussel	sea urchin
	fiddler crab	sand dollar	
	hermit crab	scallop	
Sunlight Zone	albacore	manta ray	skate
	blue marlin	octopus	sperm whale
	bluefin tuna	Portuguese man-of-war	striped dolphin
	flying fish	rattail fish	sunfish
	hermit crab	sea turtle	swordfish
	herring	sea horse	thresher shark
Twilight Zone	black devil	midwater jellyfish	viper fish
	blue shark	rattail fish	
	hatchet fish	tripod fish	
Midnight Zone	angler fish	sea cucumber	tripod fish
	black swallower	snipe eel	lantern fish
	opossum shrimp	squid	vampire squid

Save the Earth

Nobody made a greater mistake than he who did nothing because he could only do a little.

Edmund Burke

When the population of the Earth was smaller, and industrialization was restricted to a few western nations, it was possible to ignore the effects of modern life on the ecology of our planet. But ecological effects are becoming massive.

The holes in the ozone layer are increasing, our oxygen-creating rainforests are decreasing, and deserts are expanding worldwide. The children you teach today will inherit a very different Earth tomorrow if we fail to act now.

This report makes an excellent culmination to an ecology or Earth Day unit.

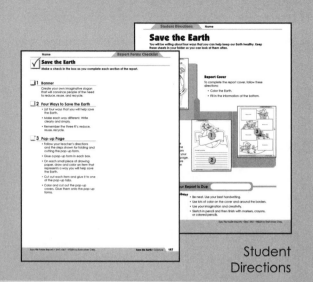

Student
Directions

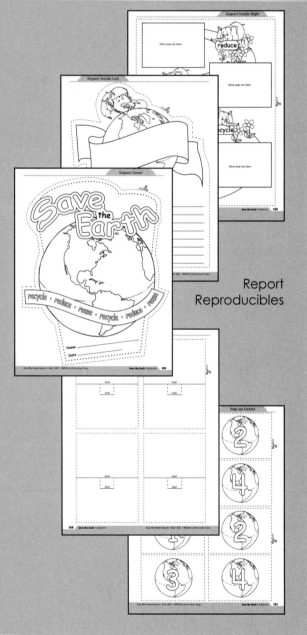

Report
Reproducibles

Before Assigning the Report

1. Prepare the following materials for each student:

   • student direction sheets on pages 146 and 147

   • report reproducibles on pages 145 and 148–151

   • 1½" (4 cm) pieces of drawing paper to draw items for the pop-up pages

2. Decide how to assign the reports. (See the directions on page 2.)

3. Conduct a class discussion about "Earth-saving" practices. List all the ideas the class thinks of. The list will be more thoughtful and complete if the discussion follows a unit of study on ecology and recycling.

Completing the Report

1. Distribute materials to students.

2. Introduce the report following the guidelines and suggestions on page 2.

3. Directions for creating the pop-ups are on page 8 and in the student directions. After students have completed page 148, you may wish to do the pop-ups together.

4. Follow the guidelines on page 3 for assisting students as they work on and complete the report.

Name _____

Date _____

Save the Earth

You will be writing about four ways that you can help keep our Earth healthy. Keep these sheets in your folder so you can look at them often.

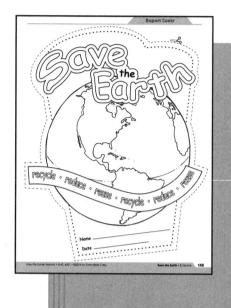

Report Cover

To complete the report cover, follow these directions:

- Color the Earth.
- Fill in the information at the bottom.

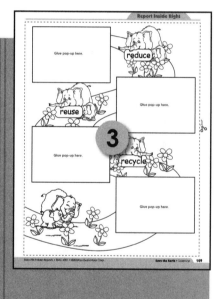

Report Forms

This diagram shows the inside of your report. The numbers on the diagram match the numbers in your directions on the next page. This is to show you where to place information on your report.

Your Report Is Due

Remember!

- Be neat. Use your best handwriting.
- Use lots of color on the cover and around the borders.
- Use your imagination and creativity.
- Sketch in pencil and then finish with markers, crayons, or colored pencils.

Save the Earth

Make a check in the box as you complete each section of the report.

1 Banner

Create your own imaginative slogan that will convince people of the need to reduce, reuse, and recycle.

2 Four Ways to Save the Earth

- List four ways that you will help save the Earth.
- Make each way different. Write clearly and simply.
- Remember the three R's: reduce, reuse, recycle.

3 Pop-up Page

- Follow your teacher's directions and the steps shown for folding and cutting the pop-up form.
- Glue a pop-up form in each box.
- On each small piece of drawing paper, draw and color an item that represents a way you will help save the Earth.
- Cut out each item and glue it to one of the pop-up tabs.
- Color and cut out the pop-up covers. Glue them onto the pop-up forms.

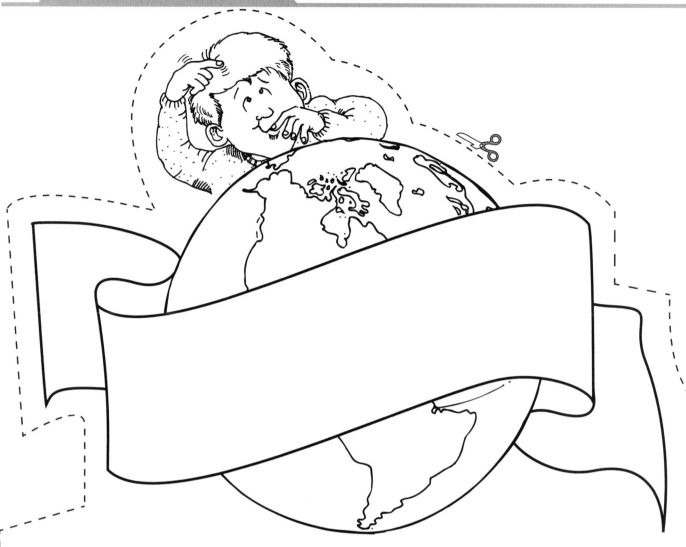

Four ways I can do this:

1. _____

_____

2. _____

_____

3. _____

_____

4. _____

_____

 Easy File Folder Reports • EMC 6001 • ©2004 by Evan-Moor Corp.

Glue pop-up here.

reduce

reuse

Glue pop-up here.

Glue pop-up here.

recycle

Glue pop-up here.

fold

fold

fold

fold

fold

fold

fold

fold

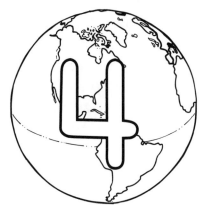

The statistics about endangered plant and animal species are frightening. According to the National Wildlife Federation:

- Plant and animal species are disappearing at least 1,000 times faster than at any other time in the last 65 million years.

- Human population growth and expansion is the biggest reason why species become extinct today; habitat loss causes about 75 percent of the extinctions occurring today.

Endangered animals need our help. Learning about endangered species is the first step in understanding the scope of the problem and developing a commitment to playing whatever roll we can to ensure the survival of the rich, abundant diversity of life on our planet.

In this report, students will research one endangered animal and learn what can be done to aid in its survival.

Endangered Animals

Easy File Folder Reports • EMC 6001 • ©2004 by Evan-Moor Corp.

Before Assigning the Report

1. Prepare the following materials for each student:

   - student direction sheets on pages 154 and 155
   - report reproducibles on pages 156–159
   - 7½" x 10" (19 x 25.5 cm) colored construction paper, for pop-up backing
   - paper for drawing endangered species for pop-up page
   - 6 sheets of plain paper, cut 4" x 7" (10 x 18 cm), for minibook
   - construction paper scraps to create a cover decoration for the minibook
   - index cards for note-taking

2. Decide how to assign the reports. (See the directions on page 2 and the list of endangered animals on page 160).

3. Discuss what it means if an animal or plant is endangered. What does *extinct* mean? Make a list of facts students know about endangered animals. Allow students to voice opinions about why certain animals may be endangered.

Completing the Report

1. Distribute materials to students.

2. Introduce the report following the guidelines and suggestions on page 2. Discuss what an interview is. Tell students that they will be writing an interview with their endangered animal. They will ask the questions and then answer them from the animal's point of view.

3. Directions for creating the pop-ups are on page 8 and in the student directions. After students have had time to research their animal, you may wish to do the pop-ups together.

4. Follow the guidelines on page 3 for assisting students as they work on and complete the report.

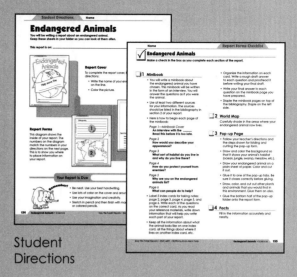

Student Directions

Report Reproducibles

Endangered Animals Reproducible

Endangered Animals

You will be writing a report about an endangered animal.
Keep these sheets in your folder so you can look at them often.

This report is on: _____

Report Cover

To complete the report cover, follow these directions:

- Write the name of your endangered animal on the top line.
- Color the picture.

Report Forms

This diagram shows the inside of your report. The numbers on the diagram match the numbers in your directions on the next page. This is to show you where to place information on your report.

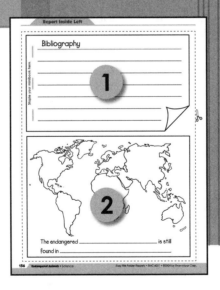

Your Report Is Due

- Be neat. Use your best handwriting.
- Use lots of color on the cover and around the borders.
- Use your imagination and creativity.
- Sketch in pencil and then finish with markers, crayons, or colored pencils.

Endangered Animals

Make a check in the box as you complete each section of the report.

☐ 1 Minibook

- You will write a minibook about the endangered animal you have chosen. This minibook will be written in the form of an interview. You will answer the questions as if you were the animal.

- Use at least two different sources for your information. The sources should be listed in the bibliography in section 2 of your report.

- Here is how to begin each page of the minibook:

  Page 1—Minibook Cover
  Write: **An interview with the _____. Read this before it is too late.**

  Page 2
  How would you describe your appearance?

  Page 3
  What sort of habitat do you live in, and why do you live there?

  Page 4
  How do you protect yourself from enemies?

  Page 5
  Why are you on the endangered animals list?

  Page 6
  What can people do to help?

- Label 5 index cards for taking notes: page 2, page 3, page 4, page 5, and page 6. Write each of the questions on the correct card. As you read your reference materials, write down information that will help you write each part of your report.

- Keep all the information about what the animal looks like on one index card, all the things about where it lives on another index card, etc.

- Organize the information on each card. Write a rough draft answer to each question and proofread it before writing your final draft.

- Write your final answer to each question on the minibook page you have prepared.

- Staple the minibook pages on top of the bibliography. Staple on the left side.

☐ 2 World Map

Carefully shade in the areas where your endangered animal now lives.

☐ 3 Pop-up Page

- Follow your teacher's directions and the steps shown for folding and cutting the pop-up form.

- Draw and color the background so that it shows your animal's habitat (ocean, jungle, swamp, meadow, etc.).

- Draw your endangered animal on a plain sheet of paper. Color and cut it out.

- Glue it to one of the pop-up tabs. Be sure it closes correctly before gluing.

- Draw, color, and cut out other plants and animals that you would find in this environment. Glue them on also.

- Glue the bottom half of the pop-up folder onto the report form.

☐ 4 Facts

Fill in the information accurately and neatly.

Bibliography

Staple your minibook here.

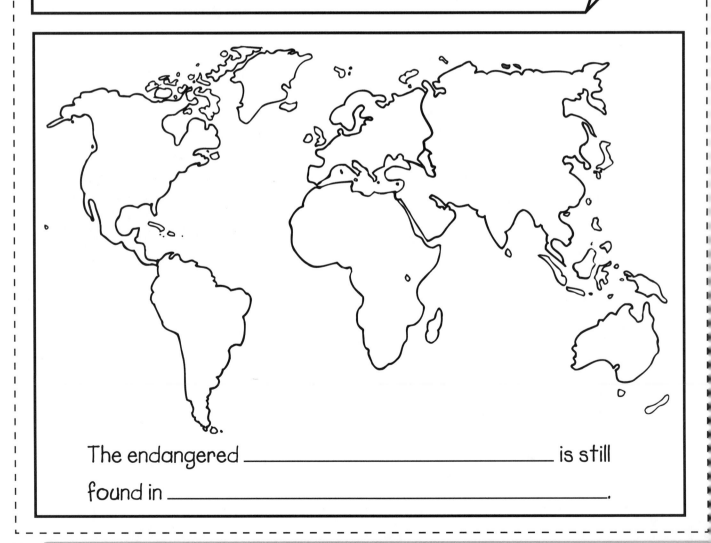

The endangered _____ is still

found in _____.

Glue the bottom half of the pop-up
page here.

Important Facts

Name: _____

Scientific Name: _____

How many are alive today? _____

Interesting facts: _____

_____

_____

Endangered Animals

Help save the _____

_____

Name: _____

Date: _____

Easy File Folder Reports • EMC 6001 • ©2004 by Evan-Moor Corp.

fold

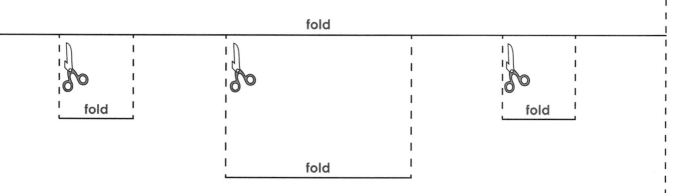

fold

fold

fold

fold

Endangered Animals

African elephant

Asian elephant

Asiatic buffalo

bighorn sheep

black swan

black-footed ferret

bottlenose dolphin

California condor

emperor penguin

emu

frilled lizard

Galápagos turtle

giant anteater

giant armadillo

giant otter

giant panda

golden parakeet

green sea turtle

Grevy's zebra

humpback whale

ibex

koala

Komodo dragon

leopard snake

Mediterranean monk seal

mountain gorilla

mustached monkey

peacock

polar bear

pygmy chimpanzee

rainbow-billed toucan

red kangaroo

scarlet macaw

snow leopard

snowy owl

Stellar sea lion

wolf

wood duck

Note: These animals and many more were on the endangered animals list in 2003. You may wish to get a more recent list and make changes as needed.

Contents

New Year's Day

Celebrating the arrival of a new year is one of the oldest holidays observed around the world. Many cultures celebrate with special foods and a big party that includes fireworks.

Cultures throughout the world associate special symbols with the new year. For example, the tradition of using an image of a baby to signify the new year began in Greece around 600 B.C. The baby symbolizes rebirth, or a "new start."

Many cultures believe that anything in the shape of a ring is good luck. The shape of a ring symbolizes "coming full circle," or completing a year's cycle. People around the world have different new year's customs and beliefs, but a common belief is that the new year is a time to think about the year that has passed and prepare for the new year that is coming.

This report will focus on plans for the new year. This is a good time for students to make a new year's resolution that will have a positive impact on their lives.

Easy File Folder Reports • EMC 6001 • ©2004 by Evan-Moor Corp.

Before Assigning the Report

Prepare the following materials for each student:

- student direction sheets on pages 164 and 165
- report reproducibles on pages 166–169
- for the pipe-cleaner persons:
  - 4" (10 cm) square piece of cardboard
  - 3 pipe cleaners
  - a variety of materials to dress and finish the characters (See page 4.)
  - 20 foil stars

Completing the Report

1. Distribute materials to students.

2. Introduce the report following the guidelines and suggestions on page 2.

3. Guide students step by step to make two pipe-cleaner people. Students will use two pipe cleaners to make the old man, representing the old year. They cut the third pipe cleaner in half to make the new year's baby (see page 4).

4. Guide students in writing the dates on the calendar (pages 167 and 168).

5. Follow the guidelines on page 3 for assisting students as they work on and complete the report.

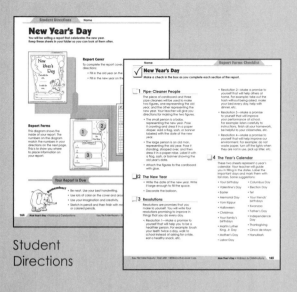

Student
Directions

Report
Reproducibles

New Year's Day

You will be writing a report that celebrates the new year.
Keep these sheets in your folder so you can look at them often.

Report Cover

To complete the report cover, follow these directions:

- Fill in the old year on the first line.
- Fill in the new year on the second line.

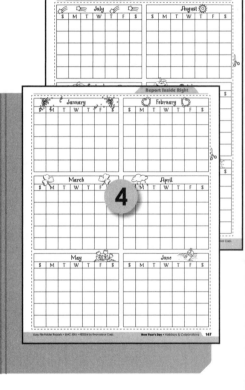

Report Forms

This diagram shows the inside of your report. The numbers on the diagram match the numbers in your directions on the next page. This is to show you where to place information on your report.

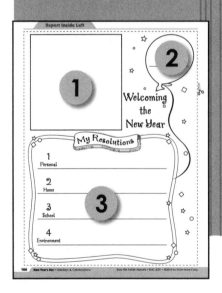

Your Report Is Due

Remember!

- Be neat. Use your best handwriting.
- Use lots of color on the cover and around the borders.
- Use your imagination and creativity.
- Sketch in pencil and then finish with markers, crayons, or colored pencils.

New Year's Day

Make a check in the box as you complete each section of the report.

1 Pipe-Cleaner People

The piece of cardboard and three pipe cleaners will be used to make two figures, one representing the old year, and the other representing the new year. Your teacher will give you directions for making the two figures.

- The small person is a baby, representing the new year. Pose it crawling and dress it in a paper diaper. Add a flag, sash, or banner labeled with the date of the new year.

- The large person is an old man, representing the old year. Pose it standing, stooped over, and then dress it in a paper robe. Label it with a flag, sash, or banner showing the old year's date.

- Attach the figures to the cardboard with glue.

2 The New Year

- Write the date of the new year. Write it large enough to fill the space.

- Decorate the balloon.

3 Resolutions

Resolutions are promises that you make to yourself. You will write four resolutions promising to improve in things that you do every day.

- Resolution 1—Make a promise to yourself that will help you to be a healthier person. For example: brush your teeth twice a day, walk to school instead of asking for a ride, eat a healthy snack, etc.

- Resolution 2—Make a promise to yourself that will help others at home. For example: take out the trash without being asked, make your bed every day, help with dinner, etc.

- Resolution 3—Make a promise to yourself that will improve your performance at school. For example: listen carefully to instructions, finish all your homework, be helpful to your classmates, etc.

- Resolution 4—Make a promise to yourself that will help improve our environment. For example: do not waste paper, turn off the lights when they are not in use, pick up litter, etc.

4 The Year's Calendar

These two sheets represent a year's calendar. Your teacher will guide you in filling in the dates. Label the important days and mark them with foil stars. Some suggestions:

- Your birthday
- Valentine's Day
- Easter
- Memorial Day
- Yom Kippur
- Halloween
- Christmas
- Your family's birthdays
- Martin Luther King, Jr. Day
- Mother's Day
- Labor Day
- Columbus Day
- Election Day
- Tet
- Your friends' birthdays
- Kwanzaa
- Father's Day
- Independence Day
- Thanksgiving
- Cinco de Mayo
- Hanukkah

Set your
pipe-cleaner person
here.

Welcoming
the
New Year

My Resolutions

1
Personal
_____

2
Home
_____

3
School
_____

4
Environment
_____

   Easy File Folder Reports • EMC 6001 • ©2004 by Evan-Moor Corp.

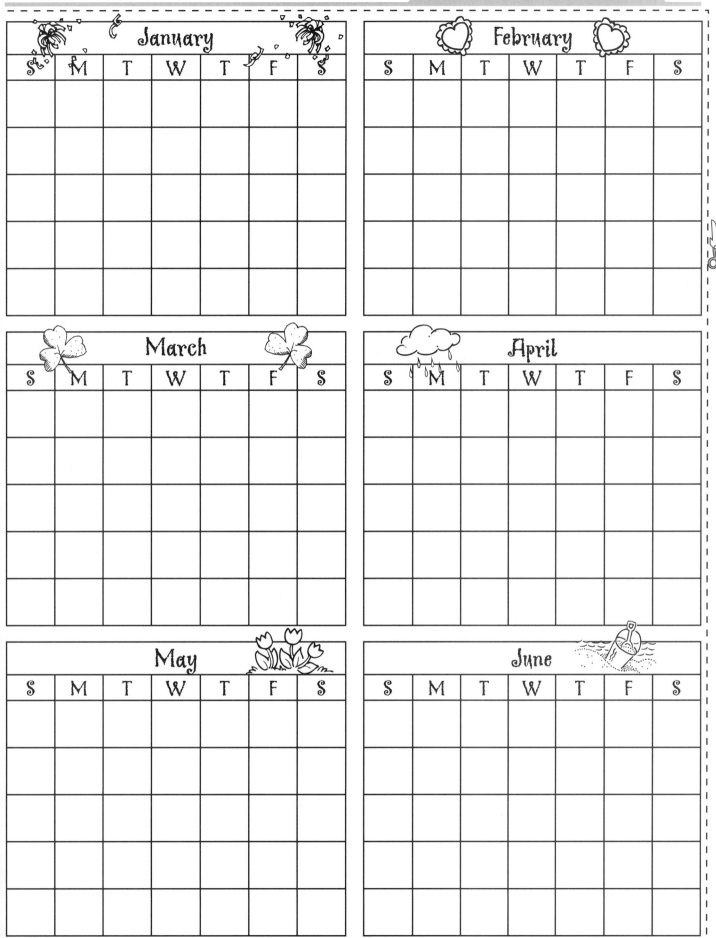

S	M	T	W	T	F	S

January

February

March

April

May

June

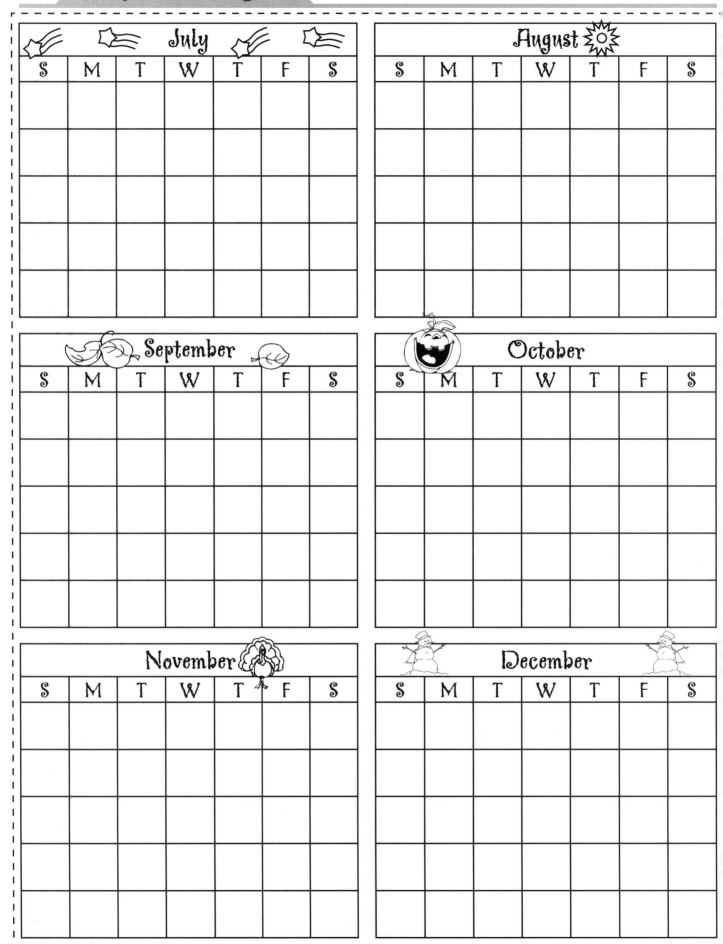

July

S	M	T	W	T	F	S

August

S	M	T	W	T	F	S

September

S	M	T	W	T	F	S

October

S	M	T	W	T	F	S

November

S	M	T	W	T	F	S

December

S	M	T	W	T	F	S

New Year's Day

Out with the old...

_____

In with the new...

_____

Date: _____

Name: _____

Chinese New Year

Gung Hay Fat Choy! "Wishing you a prosperous New Year!" Chinese New Year lasts for fifteen days and is the biggest holiday in Chinese culture. It is celebrated on the first day of the first moon in the lunar calendar, which varies from late January to mid-February. The Chinese lunar calendar is based on the cycles of the moon. It has a twelve-year cycle, and each year is named after an animal or "sign." According to Chinese folklore, horoscopes have developed around the animal signs. People are said to have the same traits as the animal of their birth year.

During the fifteen-day Chinese New Year celebration, towns and villages are decorated with colored lanterns, flowers, and brightly colored banners that have messages of new year greetings. Many festivals and parades take place throughout the celebration. Among the most spectacular are the dragon and lion dances.

In this report, students will celebrate this ancient holiday by comparing this year's traits with the year of each reporter's birth. Gung Hay Fat Choy!

Before Assigning the Report

Prepare the following materials for each student:

- student direction sheets on pages 172 and 173

- report reproducibles on pages 174–177

- two 3" x 6" (7.5 x 15 cm) pieces of red construction paper for pop-ups

- construction paper for background color

Completing the Report

1. Distribute materials to students.

2. Introduce the report following the guidelines and suggestions on page 2.

3. Directions for making pop-ups are on page 8.

4. Follow the guidelines on page 3 for assisting students as they work on and complete the report.

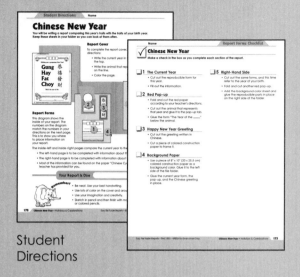

Student
Directions

The Legend of the Chinese Zodiac Animals

Long ago, 12 animals had a quarrel about who was going to be the leader in the cycle of years. To settle the argument, the 12 animals held a contest by the riverbank.

The first animal to reach the other side of the river would be the leader, and the rest would receive their years according to when they finished the race.

All of the animals jumped in the river at once and began to swim across. The big, strong ox was in the lead, but the clever rat jumped on his back. Just as the ox was about to climb onshore, the rat jumped off and won the race. The boar was the laziest of the animals, so he got to the other side last. And that is why in the Chinese cycle of years, the rat is the first year cycle, the ox second, and the boar last.

Report
Reproducibles

Chinese Cycle of Years
Reproducible

Chinese New Year

You will be writing a report comparing this year's traits with the traits of your birth year. Keep these sheets in your folder so you can look at them often.

Report Cover

To complete the report cover, follow these directions:

- Write the current year in the boxes at the top.
- Write the animal that represents this year on the first line.
- Color the page.

Report Forms

This diagram shows the inside of your report. The numbers on the diagram match the numbers in your directions on the next page. This is to show you where to place information on your report.

The inside-left and inside-right pages compare the current year to the year of your birth.

- The left-hand page should be completed with information about the current year.
- The right-hand page should be completed with information about your birth year.
- Most of the information can be found on the paper "Chinese Cycle of Years" that your teacher has provided for you.

Your Report Is Due

Remember!

- Be neat. Use your best handwriting.
- Use lots of color on the cover and around the borders.
- Use your imagination and creativity.
- Sketch in pencil and then finish with markers, crayons, or colored pencils.

Chinese New Year

Make a check in the box as you complete each section of the report.

☐ 1 The Current Year

- Cut out the reproducible form for this year.
- Fill out the information.

☐ 2 Red Pop-up

- Fold and cut the red paper according to your teacher's directions.
- Cut out the animal that represents that year and glue it to the pop-up tab.
- Glue the form "The Year of the ____" below the animal.

☐ 3 Happy New Year Greeting

- Cut out the greeting written in Chinese.
- Cut a piece of colored construction paper to frame it.

☐ 4 Background Paper

- Use a piece of 8" x 10" (20 x 25.5 cm) colored construction paper as a background color. Glue it to the left side of the file folder.
- Glue the current year form, the pop-up, and the Chinese greeting in place.

☐ 5 Right-Hand Side

- Cut out the same forms, and this time refer to the year of your birth.
- Fold and cut another red pop-up.
- Add the background color sheet and glue the reproducible parts in place on the right side of the folder.

I was born in the year

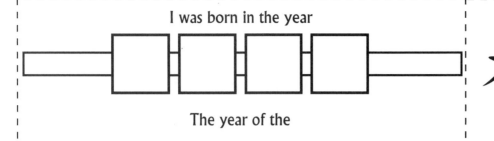

The year of the

_____

Common personality traits of those born in this year are...

_____

_____

_____

_____

恭
禧
發
財

The Year of the
_____

This is the year

The year of the

_____

Common personality traits of those born in this year are...

_____

_____

_____

_____

恭
禧
發
財

The Year of the
_____

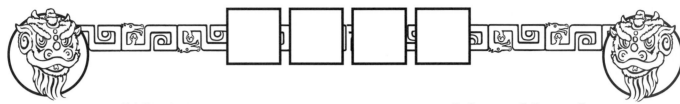

Wishing you a prosperous New Year!

Gung Hay Fat Choy

恭
禧
發
財

This is the year of the

_____

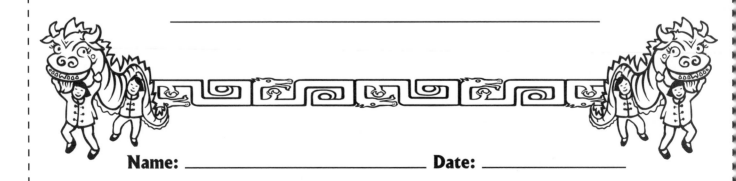

Name: _____ **Date:** _____

Chinese Cycle of Years

Year of the:		
Rat	1936, 1948, 1960, 1972, 1984, 1996, 2008, 2020	You are imaginative, charming, and very generous. You possess great personal charm, you like nice things, and you can be quick-tempered.
Ox	1937, 1949, 1961, 1973, 1985, 1997, 2009, 2021	You are a born leader. You have a calm, patient nature, and you are a good listener.
Tiger	1938, 1950, 1962, 1974, 1986, 1998, 2010, 2022	You are bold and adventurous, and have initiative and charm. You are a person of great extremes. You are a considerate friend and a bold risk taker.
Rabbit	1939, 1951, 1963, 1975, 1987, 1999, 2011, 2023	You are affectionate, cooperative, and pleasant, with a lot of friends. You are blessed with good fortune in business and games of chance.
Dragon	1940, 1952, 1964, 1976, 1988, 2000, 2012, 2024	You are a popular individual who is always full of life and enthusiasm. You have a reputation for being fun-loving, gentle, sensitive, and soft-hearted.
Snake	1941, 1953, 1965, 1977, 1989, 2001, 2013, 2025	You are a charming person who is wise and deep-thinking; intuition is your guide.
Horse	1942, 1954, 1966, 1978, 1990, 2002, 2014, 2026	You are very independent. You are a hard worker with great intelligence and drive. You are cheerful and popular.
Ram	1943, 1955, 1967, 1979, 1991, 2003, 2015, 2027	You are elegant and artistic. You are sensitive, and you appreciate artistic beauty.
Monkey	1944, 1956, 1968, 1980, 1992, 2004, 2016, 2028	You are intelligent and have a very clever wit. You have a fun-loving nature and are well-liked. You are a good decision maker, who is certain to succeed.
Rooster	1945, 1957, 1969, 1981, 1993, 2005, 2017, 2029	You are a hard worker with great decision-making skills. You are not afraid to speak your mind. You are a loyal friend.
Dog	1946, 1958, 1970, 1982, 1994, 2006, 2018, 2030	You are loyal and honest. You have a deep sense of duty and justice, and you keep secrets very well.
Boar	1947, 1959, 1971, 1983, 1995, 2007, 2019, 2031	You are sincere, tolerant, and honest. You set difficult goals and achieve them. You have a quiet inner strength, and you are courteous.

An International Report

Classrooms in the United States are filled with students from all around the world. The potential for sharing cultural differences is unparalleled. One of the purposes of this report is to help develop a dialog about people in different parts of the world.

Learning about the diversity that exists in one's own classroom is a good starting point. Have students share what they know about their own cultural heritages. Ask students about things in their homes and lifestyles that reflect their family's cultural background.

In this report, students will write about a major country in the world. Each student will research a different country and use specific information to complete the report.

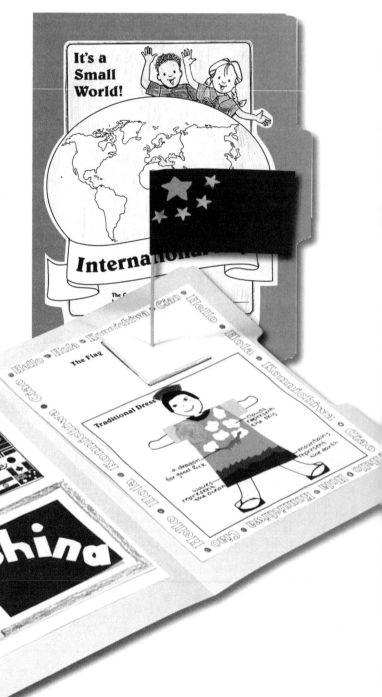

Before Assigning the Report

1. Prepare the following materials for each student:

   - student direction sheets on pages 180 and 181

   - report reproducibles on pages 182–184

   - 2½" (6.5 cm) square piece of cardboard

   - 10" (25.5 cm) bamboo skewer or straw (for a flagpole)

   - 8 sheets of plain white paper, cut 4" x 7" (10 x 18 cm)

   - colored construction paper for decorating the cover

   - 3" x 8½" (7.5 x 21.5 cm) sheet of white paper for the flag

   - construction paper or cloth scraps to use in creating the traditional costume

   - index cards for note-taking

   - foil stars

2. Decide how to assign the reports. (See the directions on page 2 and the list of World Countries on page 185.)

Completing the Report

1. Distribute materials to students.

2. Introduce the report following the guidelines and suggestions on page 2.

3. Follow the guidelines on page 3 for assisting students as they work on and complete the report.

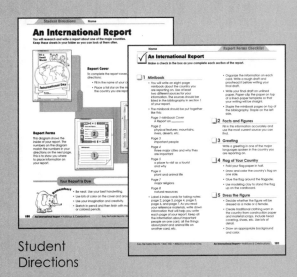

Student Directions

Report Reproducibles

World Countries Reproducible

An International Report

You will research and write a report about one of the major countries.
Keep these sheets in your folder so you can look at them often.

Report Cover

To complete the report cover, follow these directions:

- Fill in the name of your country.
- Place a foil star on the map to show where the country you are reporting on is located.

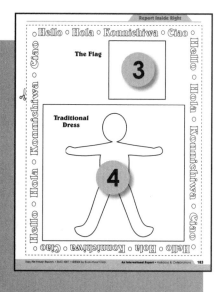

Report Forms

This diagram shows the inside of your report. The numbers on the diagram match the numbers in your directions on the next page. This is to show you where to place information on your report.

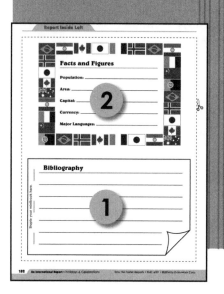

Your Report Is Due

Remember!

- Be neat. Use your best handwriting.
- Use lots of color on the cover and around the borders.
- Use your imagination and creativity.
- Sketch in pencil and then finish with markers, crayons, or colored pencils.

An International Report

Make a check in the box as you complete each section of the report.

1 Minibook

- You will write an eight-page minibook about the country you are reporting on. Use at least two different sources for your information. The sources should be listed in the bibliography in section 1 of your report.

- The minibook should be put together like this:

    Page 1–Minibook Cover
      A Report on _____

    Page 2
      physical features: mountains, rivers, deserts, etc.

    Page 3
      important people

    Page 4
      three major cities and why they are important

    Page 5
      a place to visit as a tourist and why

    Page 6
      plant and animal life

    Page 7
      major religions

    Page 8
      natural resources

- Label 6 index cards for taking notes: page 2, page 3, page 4, page 5, page 6, and page 7. As you read your reference materials, write down information that will help you write each page of your report. Keep all the information about important people on one card, all the things about plant and animal life on another card, etc.

- Organize the information on each card. Write a rough draft and proofread it before writing your final draft.

- Write your final draft on unlined paper. Paper-clip the paper on top of a lined-paper template so that your writing will be straight.

- Staple the minibook pages on top of the bibliography. Staple on the left side.

2 Facts and Figures

Fill in this information accurately and use the most current source you can find.

3 Flag of Your Country

- Fold your flag paper in half.
- Draw and color the country's flag on one side.
- Glue the flag around the flagpole.
- Use modeling clay to stand the flag up on the cardboard.

4 Dress the Figure

- Decide whether the figure will be dressed as a male or a female.

- Create traditional clothing worn in the country from construction paper and material scraps. Include head covering, shoes, etc. Use lots of detail.

- Draw an appropriate background and color.

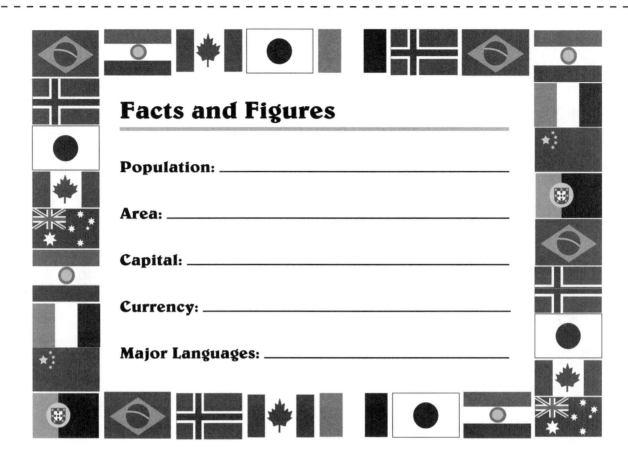

Facts and Figures

Population: _____

Area: _____

Capital: _____

Currency: _____

Major Languages: _____

Bibliography

Staple your minibook here.

_____

_____

_____

_____

_____

_____

Hello • Hola • Konnichiwa • Ciao

The Flag

Traditional Dress

It's a Small World!

International Day

The country
I am reporting on: _____

Name: _____ Date: _____

Easy File Folder Reports • EMC 6001 • ©2004 by Evan-Moor Corp.

World Countries

- Afghanistan
- Albania
- Algeria
- Andorra
- Angola
- Antigua & Barbuda
- Argentina
- Armenia
- Australia
- Austria
- Azerbaijan
- Bahamas, The
- Bahrain
- Bangladesh
- Barbados
- Belarus
- Belgium
- Belize
- Benin
- Bhutan
- Bolivia
- Bosnia and Herzegovina
- Botswana
- Brazil
- Brunei
- Bulgaria
- Burkina Faso
- Burundi
- Cambodia
- Cameroon
- Canada
- Cape Verde
- Central African Republic
- Chad
- Chile
- China
- Colombia
- Comoros
- Congo (Brazzaville)

- Congo (Kinshasa)
- Costa Rica
- Côte d'Ivoire
- Croatia
- Cuba
- Cyprus
- Czech Republic
- Denmark
- Djibouti
- Dominica
- Dominican Republic
- East Timor
- Ecuador
- Egypt
- El Salvador
- Equatorial Guinea
- Eritrea
- Estonia
- Ethiopia
- Fiji
- Finland
- France
- Gabon
- Gambia, The
- Georgia
- Germany
- Ghana
- Greece
- Grenada
- Guatemala
- Guinea
- Guinea-Bissau
- Guyana
- Haiti
- Holy City (Vatican City)
- Honduras
- Hungary
- Iceland
- India

- Indonesia
- Iran
- Iraq
- Ireland
- Israel
- Italy
- Jamaica
- Japan
- Jordan
- Kazakhstan
- Kenya
- Kiribati
- Korea, North
- Korea, South
- Kuwait
- Kyrgyzstan
- Laos
- Latvia
- Lebanon
- Lesotho
- Liberia
- Libya
- Liechtenstein
- Lithuania
- Luxembourg
- Macedonia, The former Yugoslav Republic
- Madagascar
- Malawi
- Malaysia
- Maldives
- Mali
- Malta
- Marshall Islands
- Mauritania
- Mauritius
- Mexico
- Micronesia, Federated States of
- Moldova

- Monaco
- Mongolia
- Morocco
- Mozambique
- Myanmar (Burma)
- Namibia
- Nauru
- Nepal
- Netherlands
- New Zealand
- Nicaragua
- Niger
- Nigeria
- Norway
- Oman
- Pakistan
- Palau
- Panama
- Papua New Guinea
- Paraguay
- Peru
- Philippines
- Poland
- Portugal
- Qatar
- Romania
- Russia
- Rwanda
- Saint Kitts and Nevis
- Saint Lucia
- Saint Vincent and the Grenadines
- Samoa
- San Marino
- São Tomé and Príncipe
- Saudi Arabia
- Senegal
- Serbia and Montenegro

- Seychelles
- Sierra Leone
- Singapore
- Slovakia
- Slovenia
- Solomon Islands
- Somalia
- South Africa
- Spain
- Sri Lanka
- Sudan
- Suriname
- Swaziland
- Sweden
- Switzerland
- Syria
- Tajikistan
- Tanzania
- Thailand
- Togo
- Tonga
- Trinidad and Tobago
- Tunisia
- Turkey
- Turkmenistan
- Tuvalu
- Uganda
- Ukraine
- United Arab Emirates
- United Kingdom
- United States
- Uruguay
- Uzbekistan
- Vanuatu
- Venezuela
- Vietnam
- Yemen
- Zambia
- Zimbabwe

Independence Day

Independence Day, observed on July 4th, commemorates the birthday of the United States. On July 4, 1776, the Second Continental Congress adopted the Declaration of Independence in order to declare the 13 colonies of America free from the rule of King George III of Great Britain. On July 8, 1776, with the Liberty Bell ringing, the first public reading of the Declaration of Independence took place. It announced to the world that "these United Colonies" are "Free and Independent States." Great Britain, however, did not accept this declaration peacefully. For the next eight years, the Continental Army fought in the Revolutionary War. When the war ended in 1783, the 13 victorious colonies became known as the "United States of America." That same year, Independence Day was made an official holiday. The colonies celebrated with fireworks, bonfires, military music, and, of course, by ringing the Liberty Bell. Many July 4th customs have not changed since our earliest celebrations.

Fireworks, parades, festivals, music, and picnics have all become a traditional part of America's Independence Day celebration. This report will focus on celebrating the freedom and independence that Americans enjoy.

Before Assigning the Report

1. Prepare the following materials for each student:

   - student direction sheets on pages 188 and 189

   - report reproducibles on pages 190–193

   - 3" (7.5 cm) square piece of cardboard

   - 6 sheets of plain white paper, cut 4" x 7" (10 x 18 cm)

   - skewer

   - Optional:
     –13 foil stars
     –glitter or confetti for fireworks

2. Bookmark Declaration of Independence Internet sites that are appropriate for children.

3. Provide sufficient background before students begin. You may wish to extend the lesson by posting a copy of the Declaration of Independence in your classroom. Have students define the following words, or choose some of your own. You may choose to write them on the chalkboard or prepare a worksheet.

   Write the definition of each word:

   representative: _____

   united: _____

   colony: _____

   absolved: _____

   allegiance: _____

Completing the Report

1. Distribute materials to students.

2. Introduce the report following the guidelines and suggestions on page 2.

3. Follow the guidelines on page 3 for assisting students as they work on and complete the report. This report is especially appropriate for using Internet sources or online and CD-ROM encyclopedias.

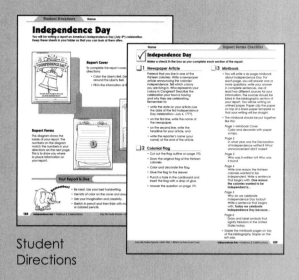

Student Directions

Report Reproducibles

Independence Day

You will be writing a report on America's Independence Day (July 4th) celebration. Keep these sheets in your folder so that you can look at them often.

Report Cover

To complete the report cover, follow these directions:

- Color the Liberty Bell. Decorate the area around the Liberty Bell.

- Fill in the information at the bottom.

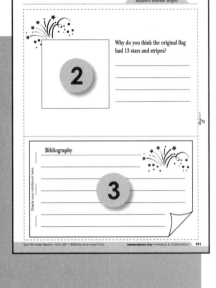

Report Forms

This diagram shows the inside of your report. The numbers on the diagram match the numbers in your directions on the next page. This is to show you where to place information on your report.

Your Report Is Due

Remember!

- Be neat. Use your best handwriting.
- Use lots of color on the cover and around the borders.
- Use your imagination and creativity.
- Sketch in pencil and then finish with markers, crayons, or colored pencils.

Independence Day

Make a check in the box as you complete each section of the report.

☐ 1 Newspaper Article

Pretend that you live in one of the thirteen colonies. Write a newspaper article announcing the colonies' independence. Tell which colony you are living in. Who represents your colony in Congress? Describe the celebration your town is having and why they are celebrating. Remember to:

- write the date on your article (use the date of the first Independence Day celebration—July 4, 1777);

- on the first line, write the name of the newspaper;

- on the second line, write the headline for your article; and

- write the reporter's name (your name) at the end of the article.

☐ 2 Colonial Flag

- Cut out the flag outline on page 193.

- Draw the original flag of the thirteen colonies.

- Color and decorate the flag.

- Glue the flag to the skewer.

- Punch a hole in the cardboard and insert the flag with a drop of glue.

- Answer the question on page 191.

☐ 3 Minibook

- You will write a six-page minibook about Independence Day. For each page, you will answer one or more questions; write your answer in complete sentences. Use at least two different sources for your information. The sources should be listed in the bibliography section of your report. You will be writing on unlined paper. Paper-clip the paper on top of a lined-paper template so that your writing will be straight.

- The minibook should be put together like this:

  Page 1—Minibook Cover
  Color and decorate with paper scraps.

  Page 2
  In what year was the Declaration of Independence written? What announcement did it make?

  Page 3
  Who was it written to? Who was it from?

  Page 4
  Write one reason the thirteen colonies wanted to be independent. Write a sentence that begins with, **One reason the colonies wanted to be independent is...**

  Page 5
  Why do we celebrate Independence Day today? Write a sentence that begins with, **Today we celebrate Independence Day because...**

  Page 6
  Draw and label symbols that signify freedom in the United States today.

- Staple the minibook pages on top of the bibliography. Staple on the left side.

Date _____

_____

_____

_____

_____

_____

_____

_____

_____

_____

_____

_____

By _____

Set your flag here.

Why do you think the original flag had 13 stars and stripes?

_____

_____

_____

_____

Bibliography

Staple your minibook here.

_____

_____

_____

_____

_____

INDEPENDENCE DAY

"Proclaim Liberty Throughout All the Land unto All the Inhabitants Thereof."

Name: _____ Date: _____

Easy File Folder Reports • EMC 6001 • ©2004 by Evan-Moor Corp.

Reproducible

Independence Day

Minibook Front Cover

Facts about the

Declaration of Independence

Pop-up Flag

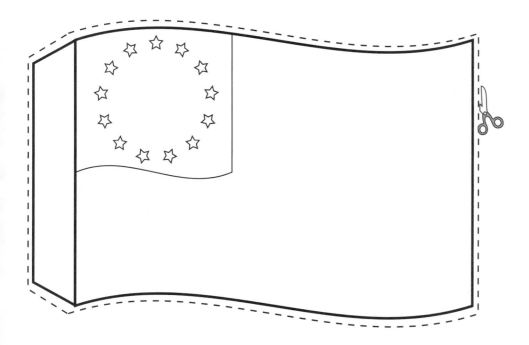

Thanksgiving Day

The late fall celebration of a plentiful harvest has come to be known as "Thanksgiving." Thanksgiving in the United States was first celebrated by the Pilgrims and Native Americans in colonial New England. The Pilgrims gave thanks for the plentiful harvest and the blessing of having survived their first year in a new land. Their first winter had been long and hard; almost half the people died. The following fall brought a good harvest, and there was reason for rejoicing. The Pilgrims were especially thankful for their Indian friends, who helped the survivors get through that first winter.

In this report, students will write about what they are thankful for. They also have the opportunity to re-create their family's Thanksgiving celebration through planning a menu and "seating guests" around their table.

Before Assigning the Report

1. Prepare the following materials for each student:

   - student direction sheets on pages 196 and 197

   - report reproducibles on pages 198–201

   - 6 sheets of plain white paper, cut 4" x 7" (10 x 18 cm)

   - assorted colored construction paper to decorate the cover of the minibook and the table setting

2. As homework, assign students the task of finding out what the Thanksgiving menu at their homes will be, and who will attend Thanksgiving dinner.

Completing the Report

1. Distribute materials to students.

2. Introduce the report following the guidelines and suggestions on page 2.

3. Follow the guidelines on page 3 for assisting students as they work on and complete the report.

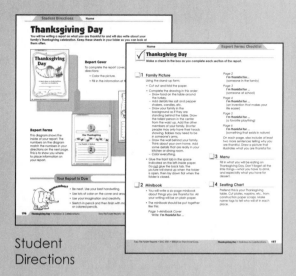

Student Directions

Report Reproducibles

Thanksgiving Day

You will be writing a report on what you are thankful for and you will also write about your family's Thanksgiving celebration. Keep these sheets in your folder so you can look at them often.

Report Cover

To complete the report cover, follow these directions:

- Color the picture.
- Fill in the information at the bottom.

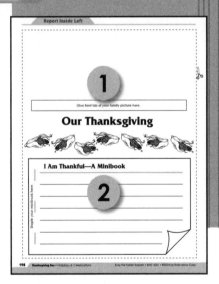

Report Forms

This diagram shows the inside of your report. The numbers on the diagram match the numbers in your directions on the next page. This is to show you where to place information on your report.

Your Report Is Due

Remember!

- Be neat. Use your best handwriting.
- Use lots of color on the cover and around the borders.
- Use your imagination and creativity.
- Sketch in pencil and then finish with markers, crayons, or colored pencils.

Thanksgiving Day

Make a check in the box as you complete each section of the report.

1 Family Picture

Using the stand-up form:

- Cut out and fold the paper.

- Complete the drawing in this order:
  - Draw food on the table around the turkey.
  - Add details like salt and pepper shakers, candles, etc.
  - Draw your family in the background as if they are standing behind the table. Draw the tallest person in the center from the waist up. Add the other members of your family. Shorter people may only have their heads showing. Babies may need to be in someone's arms.
  - Draw the wall behind your family. Think about your own home. Add some details that are really in your kitchen or dining room.
  - Color everything.

- Glue the front tab in the space indicated on the left-inside paper. Do <u>not</u> glue the back tab. The picture will stand up when the folder is open, then lay down flat when the folder is closed.

2 Minibook

- You will write a six-page minibook about things you are thankful for. All your writing will be on plain paper.

- The minibook should be put together like this:

Page 1–Minibook Cover
Write: **I'm thankful for...**

Page 2
I'm thankful for...
(someone in the family)

Page 3
I'm thankful for...
(someone at school)

Page 4
I'm thankful for...
(an invention that makes your life easier)

Page 5
I'm thankful for...
(a favorite plaything)

Page 6
I'm thankful for...
(something that exists in nature)

On each page, also include at least two more sentences telling why you are thankful. Draw a picture that illustrates what you are thankful for.

3 Menu

Fill in what you will be eating on Thanksgiving Day. Don't forget all the little things—what you have to drink, and especially what you have for dessert.

4 Seating Chart

Pretend this is your Thanksgiving table. Cut plates, napkins, etc., from construction paper scraps. Make name tags to tell who will sit in each place.

Glue front tab of your family picture here.

Our Thanksgiving

I Am Thankful—A Minibook

Staple your minibook here.

Menu

Our Thanksgiving Table

Thanksgiving Day

A report about my family traditions
and what I am thankful for.

_____

Name

_____

Date

Our Thanksgiving—Stand-up Form

back tab

fold →

← fold

fold →

← fold

fold →

← fold

front tab

December Celebrations

Welcome, December! December is full of celebrations enjoyed by different cultural groups for different reasons. Studying those differences allows students to better understand other cultures.

This report allows students to investigate six different celebrations from around the world. They will then choose one that their family celebrates and write about why it is special to them.

*My Family Celebrates—If there are students in your class who do not observe any of the December celebrations, have them write about a time that their family considers special.

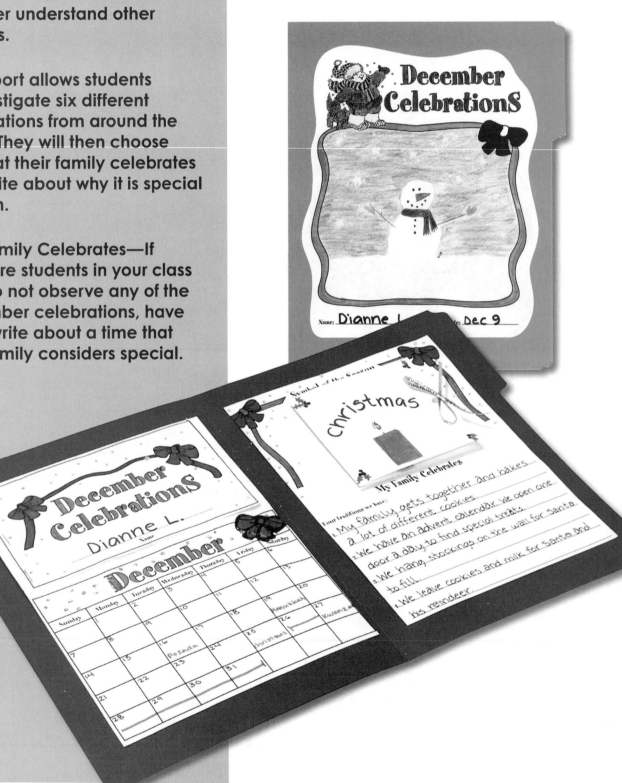

Before Assigning the Report

Prepare the following materials for each student:

- student direction sheets on pages 204 and 205
- report reproducibles on pages 206–209
- 6 sheets of plain white paper, cut 4" x 7" (10 x 18 cm)
- 4" x 18" (10 x 45.5 cm) construction paper
- festive ribbon
- index cards for note-taking

Completing the Report

1. Distribute materials to students.

2. Introduce the report following the guidelines and suggestions on page 2.

3. Follow the guidelines on page 3 for assisting students as they work on and complete the report. There are several Web sites with useful information. Instruct students to type in "December holidays" or "December celebrations" to access information on the holidays they are researching.

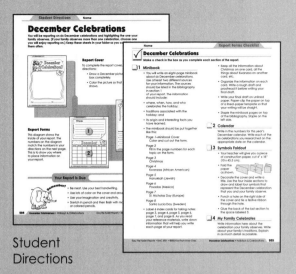

Student Directions

Report Reproducibles

December Celebrations

You will be reporting on six December celebrations and highlighting the one your family observes. (If your family observes more than one celebration, choose one you will enjoy reporting on.) Keep these sheets in your folder so you can look at them often.

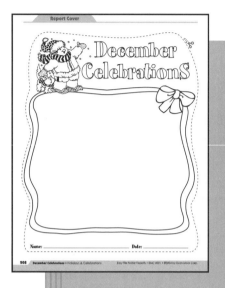

Report Cover

To complete the report cover, follow these directions:

- Draw a December picture in the box. Fill the box completely.

- Color the picture so that no white paper shows.

Report Forms

This diagram shows the inside of your report. The numbers on the diagram match the numbers in your directions on the next page. This is to show you where to place information on your report.

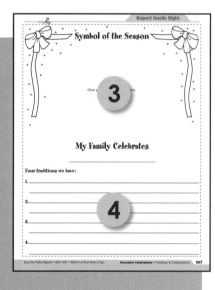

Your Report Is Due

Remember!

- Be neat. Use your best handwriting.
- Use lots of color on the cover and around the borders.
- Use your imagination and creativity.
- Sketch in pencil and then finish with markers, crayons, or colored pencils.

December Celebrations

Make a check in the box as you complete each section of the report.

☐ 1 Minibook

- You will write an eight-page minibook about six December celebrations. Use at least two different sources for your information. The sources should be listed in the bibliography in section 1 of your report. The information should include:
  - where, when, how, and who celebrates the holiday;
  - traditions associated with the holiday; and
  - its origin and interesting facts you have learned.

- The minibook should be put together like this:

  Page 1–Minibook Cover
  Color and cut out the form.

  Page 2
  Fill in the page numbers for each topic on the form.

  Page 3
  Christmas

  Page 4
  Kwanzaa (African American)

  Page 5
  Hanukkah (Jewish)

  Page 6
  Posadas (Mexico)

  Page 7
  St. Nicholas Day (Europe)

  Page 8
  Santa Lucia Day (Sweden)

- Label 6 index cards for taking notes: page 3, page 4, page 5, page 6, page 7, and page 8. As you read your reference materials, write down information that will help you write each page of your report.

- Keep all the information about Christmas on one card, all the things about Kwanzaa on another card, etc.

- Organize the information on each card. Write a rough draft and proofread it before writing your final draft.

- Write your final draft on unlined paper. Paper-clip the paper on top of a lined-paper template so that your writing will be straight.

- Staple the minibook pages on top of the bibliography. Staple on the left side.

☐ 2 Calendar

Write in the numbers for this year's December calendar. Write each of the six celebrations you researched on the appropriate date on the calendar.

☐ 3 Symbols Foldout

- Your teacher will give you a piece of construction paper, cut 4" x 18" (10 x 45.5 cm).

- Fold the paper as shown.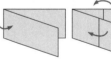

- Decorate the cover and write a title. Use the four inside sections to draw and label four symbols that represent the December celebration that you and your family observe.

- Punch a hole on the right side of the cover and tie a festive ribbon through the hole.

- Glue the back of the last section to the space labeled 3.

☐ 4 My Family Celebrates

Write information here about the celebration your family observes. Write about your family's traditions. Explain in as much detail as possible.

Bibliography

Staple your minibook here.

December

Sunday	Monday	Tuesday	Wednesday	Thursday	Friday	Saturday

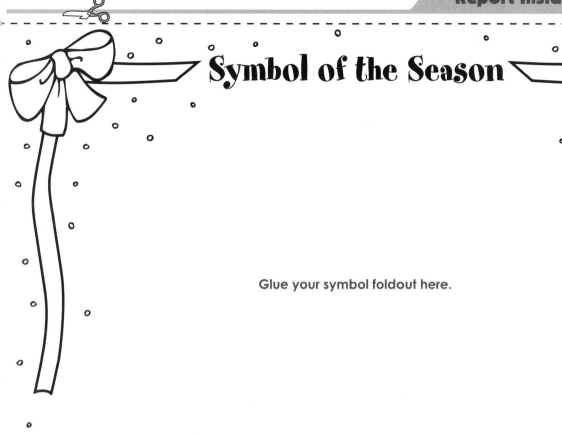

Symbol of the Season

Glue your symbol foldout here.

My Family Celebrates

_____

Four traditions we have:

1. _____

_____

2. _____

_____

3. _____

_____

4. _____

_____

December Celebrations

Name: _____ Date: _____

Cover: Color and cut it out. Fill in your name. It will be the top page.

December Celebrations

_____
Name

Second Page: Fill in the page numbers when you are completely finished.

Table of Contents

Christmas . . . . ◯

Kwanzaa . . . . ◯

Hanukkah . . . . ◯

Posadas . . . . ◯

St. Nicholas Day . . . . ◯

Santa Lucia Day . . . . ◯

Grandparents' Day

Grandparents' Day is celebrated on the second Sunday of September. It is a great time to remind your students about the importance of their grandparents. Setting aside this day gives us an opportunity to let grandparents know how much they are needed and loved, and how much wisdom, strength, and guidance they offer.

In this report, students will be interviewing a grandparent, even a "borrowed" one if theirs is not available, and sharing their ideas together. Please provide enough time for the interview to be completed in person, on the phone, or through the mail. Invite local grandparents in to see the results. They will be honored and impressed.

Decide when to assign the homework sheet (page 218). The homework sheet must be completed and returned to school before you can proceed.

Before Assigning the Report

1. Prepare the following materials for each student:

   - student direction sheets on pages 212 and 213

   - report reproducibles on pages 214–217

   - homework reproducible on page 218

   - 7½" x 10" (19 x 25.5 cm) colored construction paper

   - 3 pieces of white drawing paper, cut 3" x 4½" (7.5 x 11.5 cm)

   - 11 sheets of plain white paper, cut 4" x 7" (10 x 18 cm)

   - scraps of construction paper to decorate the minibook

2. Introduce the topic.

3. Depending on the ability of your students to follow the directions, consider cutting and folding the pop-up page as a whole class activity.

Completing the Report

1. Distribute materials to students.

2. Introduce the report following the guidelines and suggestions on page 2.

3. Explain to students that they will be reporting facts about their family.

4. Directions for making pop-ups are on page 8. You may wish to allow time in class to work on reports and materials to complete the pop-up page.

5. Follow the guidelines on page 3 for assisting students as they work on and complete the report. This report cannot be completed without the homework page.

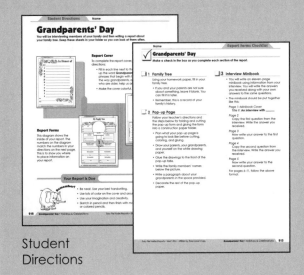

Student Directions

Report Reproducibles

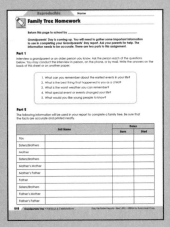

Homework Reproducible

Grandparents' Day

You will be interviewing members of your family and then writing a report about your family tree. Keep these sheets in your folder so you can look at them often.

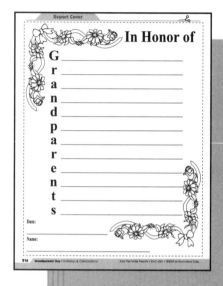

Report Cover

To complete the report cover, follow these directions:

- Fill in each line next to the letters that make up the word **Grandparents**. Use words or phrases that begin with each letter to describe the way grandparents, or people we know who are older, help us and what they give us.

- Make the cover colorful.

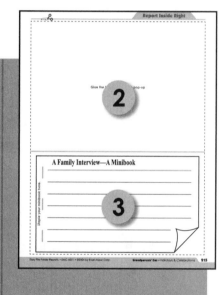

Report Forms

This diagram shows the inside of your report. The numbers on the diagram match the numbers in your directions on the next page. This is to show you where to place information on your report.

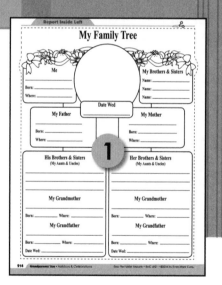

Your Report Is Due

Remember!

- Be neat. Use your best handwriting.
- Use lots of color on the cover and around the borders.
- Use your imagination and creativity.
- Sketch in pencil and then finish with markers, crayons, or colored pencils.

Name

Grandparents' Day

Make a check in the box as you complete each section of the report.

1 Family Tree

Using your homework paper, fill in your family tree.

- If you and your parents are not sure about something, leave it blank. You can fill it in later.

- Remember, this is a record of your family's history.

2 Pop-up Page

Follow your teacher's directions and the steps below for folding and cutting the pop-up form and gluing the form into a construction paper folder.

- Plan what your pop-up page is going to look like before cutting, coloring, and gluing.

- Draw your parents, your grandparents, and yourself on the white drawing paper.

- Glue the drawings to the front of the pop-up tabs.

- Write the family members' names below the picture.

- Write a paragraph about your grandparents in the space provided.

- Decorate the rest of the pop-up paper.

3 Interview Minibook

- You will write an eleven-page minibook using information from your interview. You will write the answers you received along with your own answers to the same questions.

- The minibook should be put together like this:

Page 1–Minibook Cover
Title it: **An Interview with** _____

Page 2
Copy the first question from the interview. Write the answer you received.

Page 3
Now write your answer to the first question.

Page 4
Copy the second question from the interview. Write the answer you received.

Page 5
Now write your answer to the second question.

For pages 6–11, follow the above format.

My Family Tree

Me

_____

Born: _____

Where: _____

My Brothers & Sisters

Name: _____

Name: _____

Name: _____

Date Wed

_____

My Father

_____

Born: _____

Where: _____

My Mother

_____

Born: _____

Where: _____

His Brothers & Sisters
(My Aunts & Uncles)

_____

_____

_____

My Grandmother

_____

Born: _____ Where: _____

My Grandfather

_____

Born: _____ Where: _____

Date Wed: _____

Her Brothers & Sisters
(My Aunts & Uncles)

_____

_____

_____

My Grandmother

_____

Born: _____ Where: _____

My Grandfather

_____

Born: _____ Where: _____

Date Wed: _____

 Easy File Folder Reports • EMC 6001 • ©2004 by Evan-Moor Corp.

Glue the bottom half of the pop-up
page here.

A Family Interview—A Minibook

Staple your minibook here.

In Honor of

Grandparents

_____

_____

_____

_____

_____

_____

_____

_____

_____

_____

Date:

_____

Name:

_____

Celebrate Grandparents' Day!

fold

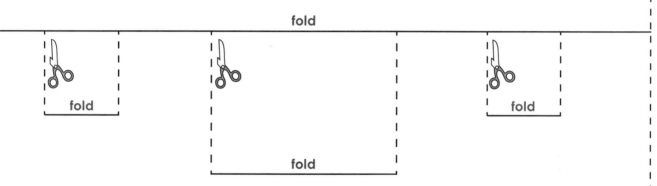

fold

fold

fold

fold

My favorite thing about having grandparents is:

_____

_____

_____

_____

Family Tree Homework

Return this page to school by _____.

Grandparents' Day is coming up. You will need to gather some important information to use in completing your Grandparents' Day report. Ask your parents for help. The information needs to be accurate. There are two parts to this assignment.

Part 1

Interview a grandparent or an older person you know. Ask the person each of the questions below. You may conduct the interview in person, on the phone, or by mail. Write the answers on the back of this sheet or on another paper.

1. What can you remember about the earliest events in your life?
2. What is the best thing that happened to you as a child?
3. What is the worst weather you can remember?
4. What special event or events changed your life?
5. What would you like young people to know?

Part 2

The following information will be used in your report to complete a family tree. Be sure that the facts are accurate and printed neatly.

Full Name	Dates	
	Born	**Died**
You		
Sisters/Brothers		
Mother		
Sisters/Brothers		
Mother's Mother		
Mother's Father		
Father		
Sisters/Brothers		
Father's Mother		
Father's Father		

Arbor Day

Arbor Day is a day designated for planting trees. The word *arbor* comes from the word *arboriculture*, which means "the cultivation of trees and shrubs." Arbor Day was first celebrated in Nebraska on April 10, 1872. The idea began with a man named Julius Sterling Morton, who as a young boy, always lived where there were great forests. After finishing college, Morton moved to Nebraska, and for the first time he saw land without any trees. He missed trees and talked to government officials about planting trees in Nebraska. People agreed to help and set aside April 10th for this day. Today, Nebraska celebrates Arbor Day on April 22nd, Morton's birthday. By proclamation, National Arbor Day is the last Friday in April. Arbor Day, however, is observed on different days in different states—a date when the state's climate is suitable for planting.

With this report, you and your students can celebrate Arbor Day, while learning about the parts of trees and their functions.

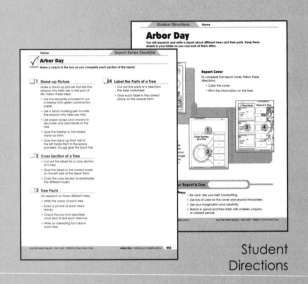

Student
Directions

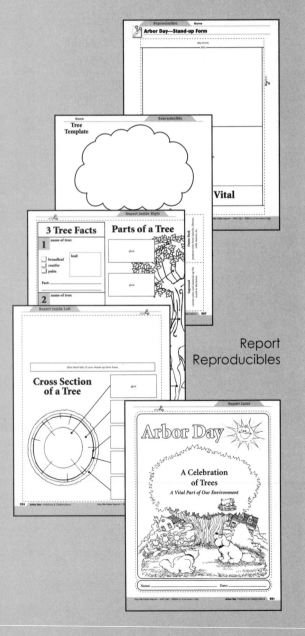

Report
Reproducibles

Before Assigning the Report

Prepare the following materials for each student:

- student direction sheets on pages 222 and 223
- report reproducibles on pages 221 and 224–227
- 6" x 8" (15 x 20 cm) green construction paper

Completing the Report

1. Distribute materials to students.

2. Introduce the report following the guidelines and suggestions on page 2.

3. Gather resources that students can use to learn about the parts of a tree.

4. Directions for making a stand-up visual are on page 6.

5. Follow the guidelines on page 3 for assisting students as they work on and complete the report.

Arbor Day

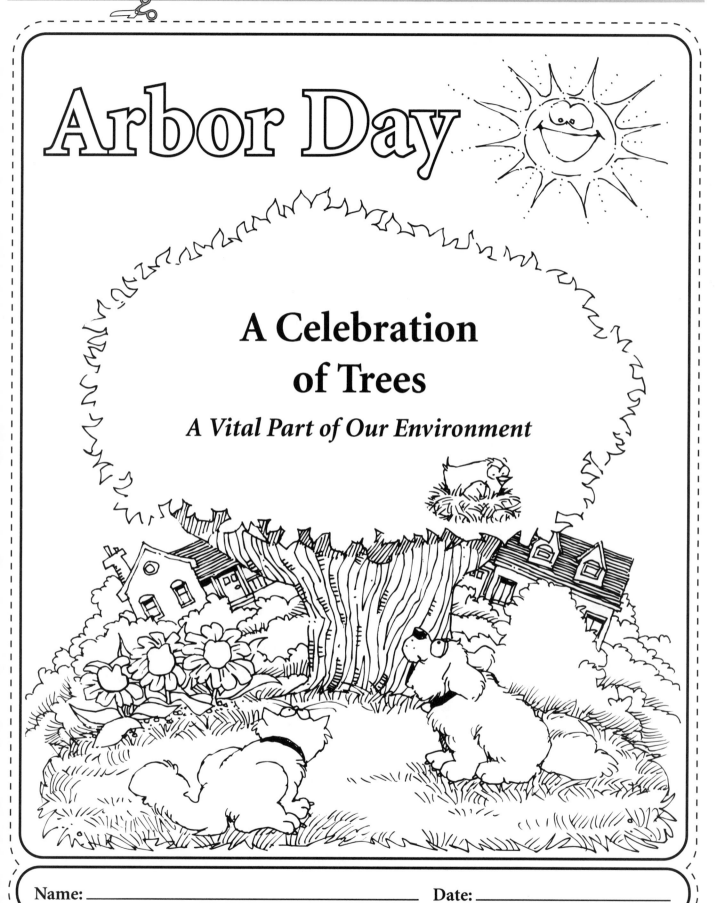

A Celebration
of Trees

A Vital Part of Our Environment

Name: _____ Date: _____

Arbor Day

You will be researching and writing a report about different trees and their parts. Keep these sheets in your folder so you can look at them often.

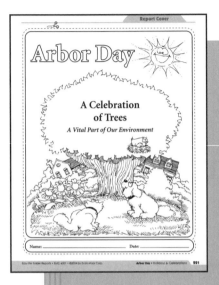

Report Cover

To complete the report cover, follow these directions:

- Color the cover.
- Fill in the information on the lines.

Report Forms

This diagram shows the inside of your report. The numbers on the diagram match the numbers in your directions on the next page. This is to show you where to place information on your report.

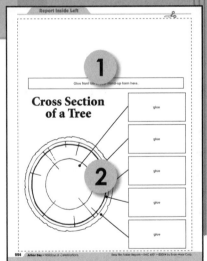

Your Report Is Due

Remember!

- Be neat. Use your best handwriting.
- Use lots of color on the cover and around the borders.
- Use your imagination and creativity.
- Sketch in pencil and then finish with markers, crayons, or colored pencils.

Arbor Day

Make a check in the box as you complete each section of the report.

☐ 1 Stand-up Picture

Make a stand-up picture that lists five reasons why trees are a vital part of life. Follow these steps:

- Use the template provided to cut a treetop from green construction paper.

- Use a black marking pen to write five reasons why trees are vital.

- Use paper scraps and crayons to decorate and add details to the tree.

- Glue the treetop to the folded stand-up form.

- Glue the stand-up front tab to the left inside form in the space provided. Do <u>not</u> glue the back tab.

☐ 2 Cross Section of a Tree

- Cut out the labels for a cross section of a tree.

- Glue the labels in the correct boxes on the left side of the report form.

- Color the cross section to emphasize the different layers.

☐ 3 Tree Facts

Do research on three different trees.

- Write the name of each tree.

- Draw a picture of each tree's leaves.

- Check the box that describes what kind of leaf each tree has.

- Write an interesting fact about each tree.

☐ 4 Parts of a Tree

- Cut out the parts of a tree from the trees worksheet.

- Glue each label in the correct place on the answer form.

Glue front tab of your stand-up form here.

Cross Section of a Tree

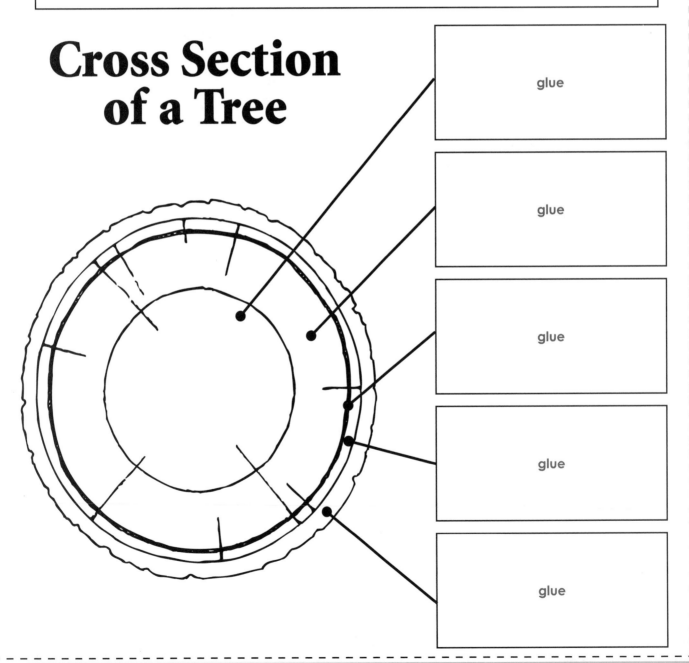

glue

glue

glue

glue

glue

Easy File Folder Reports • EMC 6001 • ©2004 by Evan-Moor Corp.

3 Tree Facts

1 name of tree: _____

☐ broadleaf
☐ conifer
☐ palm

leaf:

Fact: _____
_____

2 name of tree: _____

☐ broadleaf
☐ conifer
☐ palm

leaf:

Fact: _____
_____

3 name of tree: _____

☐ broadleaf
☐ conifer
☐ palm

leaf:

Fact: _____
_____

Parts of a Tree

glue

glue

glue

glue

glue

Reproducible

Arbor Day—Stand-up Form

back tab

— fold —

— fold —

Glue the tree here.

Trees Are Vital

— fold —

front tab

Tree Template

Parts of a Tree

Leaves
conduct photosynthesis—a process in which carbon dioxide, water, and energy from sunlight combine to make sugar that feeds the tree; breathe out oxygen

Trunk
supports the branches and leaves and carries food and water throughout the tree

Branches
grow out from the trunk; together with the twigs and leaves, form the crown of the tree

Tap Root
the biggest root; grows straight down, deep into the ground

Roots
anchor the tree in the ground; take in water and minerals from the ground and pass them up to the branches and leaves

Cross Section of a Tree

Cambium
single layer of cells between the inner bark and the sapwood; where growth happens

Inner Bark
carries food made in leaves to the rest of tree

Outer Bark
protects trees from injuries, disease, cold, insects, etc.

Heartwood
older sapwood in the center of the tree

Sapwood
carries water and minerals up the trunk to the leaves

With this report, students have a chance to research their own birth date. They will make a pipe-cleaner person showing their special characteristics, complete a birth certificate, and learn about the symbols that represent their individual birthdays. The final product is a tribute to individual uniqueness. After completing this report, take the opportunity to have one big birthday party!

Birthdays

Decide when to assign the homework sheet (page 237). The homework sheet must be completed and returned to school before you can proceed.

Before Assigning the Report

1. Prepare the following materials for each student:

   - student direction sheets on pages 230 and 231

   - report reproducibles on pages 232–236

   - homework reproducible on page 237

   - 4" (10 cm) square piece of cardboard

   - 2 pipe cleaners

2. Gather resources where students can find persons born on their birthday. An Internet search for "birthdays of famous people" will turn up a number of sites.

Completing the Report

1. Distribute materials to students.

2. Introduce the report following the guidelines and suggestions on page 2.

3. Guide students step by step to make the pipe-cleaner person (see page 4).

4. Follow the guidelines on page 3 for assisting students as they work on and complete the report.

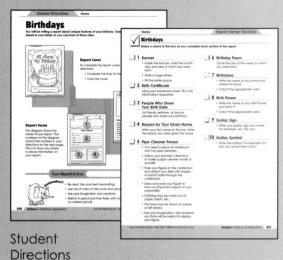

Student Directions

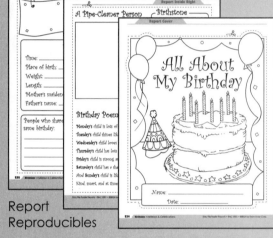

Report Reproducibles

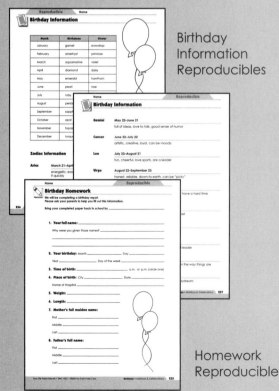

Birthday Information Reproducibles

Homework Reproducible

Birthdays

You will be writing a report about unique features of your birthday. Keep these sheets in your folder so you can look at them often.

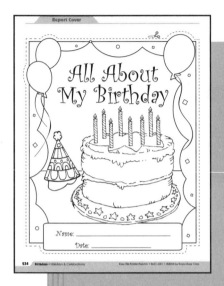

Report Cover

To complete the report cover, follow these directions:

- Complete the lines at the bottom.
- Color the cover.

Report Forms

This diagram shows the inside of your report. The numbers on the diagram match the numbers in your directions on the next page. This is to show you where to place information on your report.

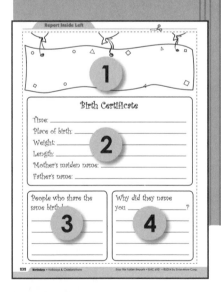

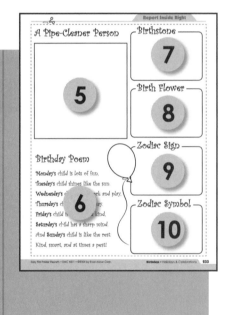

Your Report Is Due

Remember!

- Be neat. Use your best handwriting.
- Use lots of color on the cover and around the borders.
- Use your imagination and creativity.
- Sketch in pencil and then finish with markers, crayons, or colored pencils.

Birthdays

Make a check in the box as you complete each section of the report.

1 Banner

- Inside the banner, write the month, day, and year in which you were born.
- Write in large letters.
- Fill the entire space.

2 Birth Certificate

Using your homework sheet, fill in the information requested.

3 People Who Share Your Birth Date

List friends, relatives, or famous people who share your birthday.

4 Reason for Your Given Name

Write your first name on the line. Write the reason you were given this name.

5 Pipe-Cleaner Person

- You need a piece of cardboard and two pipe cleaners.
- Follow your teacher's directions to make a pipe-cleaner model of yourself.
- Pose your figure on the cardboard and attach your feet with staples, or punch holes through the cardboard.
- Dress and pose your figure to show an important aspect of your personality.
- Clothing may be made out of paper, fabric, etc.
- The face may be drawn on paper or left empty.
- Use your imagination. Use whatever you think will be helpful to display your figure.

6 Birthday Poem

Circle the day of the week on which you were born.

7 Birthstone

- Write the name of your stone and where it is found.
- Color it the appropriate color.

8 Birth Flower

- Write the name of your birth flower and draw it.
- Color it the appropriate color.

9 Zodiac Sign

- Write your zodiac sign and name. For example: Leo, the Lion

10 Zodiac Symbol

- Draw the symbol. For example: for Leo, you would draw a lion.

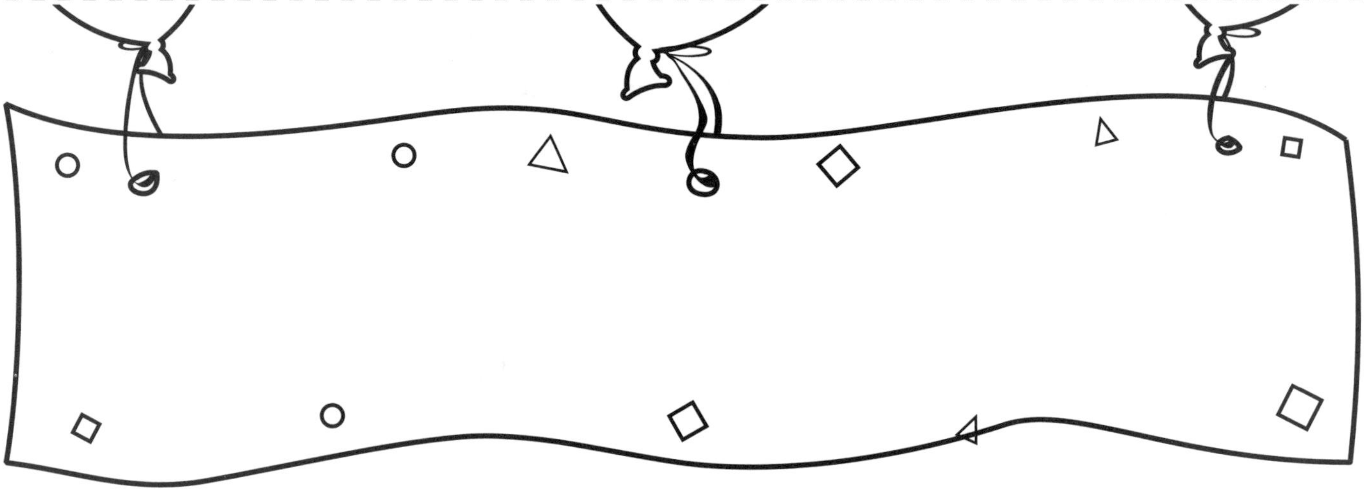

Birth Certificate

Time: _____

Place of birth: _____

Weight: _____

Length: _____

Mother's maiden name: _____

Father's name: _____

People who share the same birthday:

_____

_____

_____

_____

Why did they name you _____?

_____

_____

_____

_____

   Easy File Folder Reports • EMC 6001 • ©2004 by Evan-Moor Corp.

A Pipe-Cleaner Person

Birthstone

Birth Flower

Zodiac Sign

Zodiac Symbol

Birthday Poem

Monday's child is lots of fun,

Tuesday's child shines like the sun.

Wednesday's child loves work and play,

Thursday's child has lots to say.

Friday's child is strong and kind,

Saturday's child has a sharp mind.

And Sunday's child is like the rest:

Kind, smart, and at times a pest!

All About My Birthday

Name: _____

Date: _____

Birthday Information

Month	Birthstone	Flower
January	garnet	snowdrop
February	amethyst	primrose
March	aquamarine	violet
April	diamond	daisy
May	emerald	hawthorn
June	pearl	rose
July	ruby	waterlily
August	peridot	poppy
September	sapphire	morning glory
October	opal	hops
November	topaz	chrysanthemum
December	turquoise	holly

Zodiac Information

Aries **March 21–April 20**

energetic; easily excited; fun-loving; you get mad fast, but get over it quickly

Taurus **April 21–May 21**

like quieter activities, can be stubborn, like to make up your own mind about doing things

Birthday Information

Gemini   **May 22–June 21**

full of ideas, love to talk, good sense of humor

Cancer   **June 22–July 22**

artistic, creative, loyal, can be moody

Leo   **July 23–August 21**

fun, cheerful, love sports, are a leader

Virgo   **August 22–September 23**

honest, reliable, down-to-earth, can be "picky"

Libra   **September 24–October 23**

smart, artistic, get along with everyone, may have a hard time making up your mind

Scorpio   **October 24–November 22**

mysterious, emotional, loyal, can keep a secret

Sagittarius   **November 23–December 22**

funny, smart, adventurous, love animals

Capricorn   **December 23–January 20**

down-to-earth, mature, like school, a natural leader

Aquarius   **January 21–February 19**

smart, friendly, a quick thinker, like to question the way things are

Pisces   **February 20–March 20**

sensitive, have a lively imagination, like to daydream

Reproducible

Birthday Homework

We will be completing a birthday report.
Please ask your parents to help you fill out this information.

Bring your completed paper back to school by _____.

1. Your full name: _____

Why were you given those names? _____

_____

_____

2. Your birthday: Month _____ Day _____

Year _____ Day of the week _____

3. Time of birth: _____ a.m. or p.m. (circle one)

4. Place of birth: City _____ State _____

Name of Hospital _____

5. Weight: _____

6. Length: _____

7. Mother's full maiden name:

First _____

Middle _____

Last _____

8. Father's full name:

First _____

Middle _____

Last _____

Reproducible

Student Proofreading Checklist

Use this checklist to review and revise your writing:

☐	Does each sentence begin with a capital letter?
☐	Do names of people and places begin with a capital letter?
☐	Does each sentence end with a period, a question mark, or an exclamation point?
☐	Did I use apostrophes to show possession (Ana's desk) and in contractions (isn't)?
☐	Did I choose the correct word (to, too, two)?
☐	Did I check for spelling errors?
☐	Did I place commas where they are needed?
☐	Are my sentences clear and complete?

☐	Does each sentence begin with a capital letter?
☐	Do names of people and places begin with a capital letter?
☐	Does each sentence end with a period, a question mark, or an exclamation point?
☐	Did I use apostrophes to show possession (Ana's desk) and in contractions (isn't)?
☐	Did I choose the correct word (to, too, two)?
☐	Did I check for spelling errors?
☐	Did I place commas where they are needed?
☐	Are my sentences clear and complete?

How to Write a Bibliography Entry

Book

Author (Last name, First name). <u>Title</u>. Place: Publisher, date.

Example:

Smith, John. <u>Native Americans</u>. New York: Best Books Press, 2004.

Encyclopedia

"Article title." <u>Encyclopedia</u>. Date.

Example:

"Abraham Lincoln." <u>The New Children's Encyclopedia</u>. 2004.

Videotape

<u>Title</u>. Videotape. Production Company, date.

Example:

<u>Yellowstone National Park</u>. Videotape. Around Our Land Co., 2004.

CD-ROM

"Article title" CD-ROM. <u>CD-ROM Title</u>. Publisher, date.

Example:

"Martin Luther King, Jr." CD-ROM. <u>The Best Electronic Encyclopedia</u>. Hometown Publishing, 2004.